DIANA

THE UNTOLD STORY

DIANA

THE UNTOLD STORY

Richard Kay & Geoffrey Levy

TED SMART

First published in partwork format in Great Britain in 1998 by the *Daily Mail*

This edition published for The Book People 1998
Hall Wood Avenue
Haydock
St Helens
WA11 9UL

Associated companies throughout the world

ISBN 0 7522 2172 8

Fashion features in Chapter Ten, 'Fashion Icon' on pages
97–99, 102–107 written by Brenda Polan.

9 8 7 6 5 4 3 2 1

A CIP catalogue record for this book is available from the British Library.

Designed and typeset by Blackjacks
Printed and bound in Great Britain by The Bath Press

CONTENTS

INTRODUCTION

BY RICHARD KAY

On Saturday 30 August 1997, six hours before the Princess of Wales and the man she loved were killed in a *paparazzi* car chase, she telephoned me from Paris.

She told me she had decided to radically change her life. She was going to complete her obligations to her charities and to the anti-personnel landmines cause and then, around November, would completely withdraw from her formal public life.

She would then, she said, be able to live as she always wanted to live. Not as an icon – how she hated to be called one – but as a private person. It was a dream sequence I'd heard from her before, but this time I knew she meant it.

In my view, as someone close to the Princess for almost five years, Dodi Al Fayed was a significant factor in that decision. She was in love with him and, perhaps more important, she believed that he was in love with her and that he believed in her. They were, to use an old but price-less cliché, blissfully happy. I cannot say for certain that they would have married, or that it was even likely, but it was certainly possible.

None of this would mean an end to the good works that had become so closely identified with her, she explained. Dodi's father, Mohamed Al Fayed, had

agreed to help finance a charity for the victims of land mines and, with Dodi's encouragement, she also had sketched out the framework of a plan to open hospices for the dying all over the world.

And yet, in the midst of all this excitement, she suddenly said: 'But I sometimes wonder, what's the point? Whatever I do, it's never good enough for some people.' There was a sigh and a silence. At the other end of the line was not so much a Princess as a little girl who had unburdened herself and was in need of words of comfort and understanding.

She knew that whatever I said and whatever I might write, it would always be what I thought; and sometimes, necessarily, it would be critical.

For that reason she trusted me and revealed herself constantly as a person completely unrecognizable to her most vocal critics, many of whom had never even met her. They saw a scheming manipulator, a plotter, shrieking for attention and demanding the world's approval and indulgence.

I knew a girl of utter simplicity – even naïvety – frightened, uncertain and, as Tony Blair said in his moving tribute in the immediate aftermath of her death, who was delightful company, especially when off duty.

(Above): *Diana with shy toddler Harry on holiday in Majorca with the Spanish royal family in August 1986.*
(Opposite): *The 30-year-old Princess looking tanned, healthy and happy in this beautiful picture from 1991.*

*After the painful walk down St Paul's
625ft aisle, Earl Spencer proudly hands
over his daughter to the care of Prince Charles.*

In our final telephone conversation on that Saturday she asked me why the media were 'so anti-Dodi'. 'Is it because he's a millionaire?' she suggested hesitantly. You cannot be a 'manipulator' and ask a serious question like that.

Anyway, I told her it had nothing to do with his money and was more involved with his father's controversial image.

She listened. 'Hmm.' Maybe for once she thought I was being diplomatically evasive. It seemed to me that she actually believed that in a world filled with the disadvantaged, being rich might be something to be ashamed of.

But this was a Princess who understood so little about this aspect of the real world she left behind when she married in 1981 that the first time she insisted on paying for two coffees in an anonymous café where we had met for a chat, away from prying eyes, she tried to leave a £5 tip on top of a £2 bill.

Suddenly she brightened and we switched subjects to her 'boys', William and Harry.

'I'm coming home tomorrow and the boys will be back from Scotland in the evening,' she said. 'I will have a few days with them before they're back at school.' It may sound thoroughly irrelevant to reiterate what was obvious to everyone, her devotion to her sons, but the significance lay in their uncomplicated love for her.

She was a bit troubled on Saturday because William had called her to say that he was being required by Buckingham Palace to 'perform' – they wanted him to carry out a photo call at Eton where he was due to begin his third year on Wednesday.

What troubled Diana, and indeed William, was that the spotlight was being shone exclusively on William, fifteen, and not his 12-year-old brother Harry. She had told me on a previous occasion how hard it was for Harry as a second son being overshadowed by William, and said she tried to ensure as far as possible that everything was shared; a point endorsed by Prince Charles.

In her two sons – and latterly in Dodi – she saw the only men in her life who had never let her down and never wanted from her anything except her being herself.

It was on a return flight from Nepal early in 1993 that the Princess and I had our first serious and lengthy conversation. We had a number of mutual friends and I had met her on several previous occasions. We talked about her trip, her children, her family and mine.

It was the start of what became a friendship based on one crucial element: her complete understanding that I, as a journalist, would never sacrifice my impartiality, especially where it concerned her acrimonious differences with the Prince of Wales and certain members of the Royal Family.

Competitors and some royal advisers frequently suggested that I was in her pocket, a view which was encouraged by that now well-known picture of me getting out of her car in Beauchamp Place, Knightsbridge – snapped, inevitably, by a *paparazzo*.

Over the years I saw her at her happiest and in her darkest moments. There were moments of confusion and despair when I believed Diana was being driven by the incredible pressures made on her almost to the point of destruction.

I knew from the outset that her land mines campaign would cause her as much distress as satisfaction. Diana's simple notion of using her own fame to save lives was thrown back in her face by politicians who accused the Princess of embarrassing the Government by meddling in

*The Princess of Wales with her sons
at Highgrove in August 1988.*

things she didn't fully understand. 'What is there to understand when people are having their legs blown off?' she asked me on many occasions.

She talked of being strengthened by events, and anyone could see how the 20-year-old bride had grown into a mature woman, but I never found her strong. She was as unsure of herself at her death as when I first talked with her on that airplane and she wanted reassurance about the role she was creating for herself.

In private she was a completely different person from the manicured clothes horse that the public's insatiable demand for icons had created. She was natural and witty and did a wonderful impression of the Queen. This was the person, she told me, that she would have been all the time if she hadn't married into the world's most famous family.

Just before Diana's last Christmas I lunched with her at a friend's house in Hampstead. We ate vegetable curry, with pulses and rice, and drank still water. Diana was intoxicating company. She never needed on that day – or

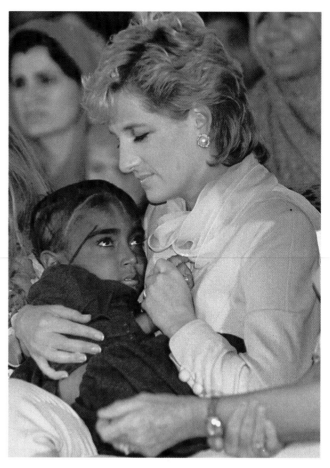

(Right): *Diana embracing a young patient at a cancer hospital in Lahore, Pakistan in August 1996.* (Below): *With a sick toddler in Lahore, Pakistan in February 1996.*

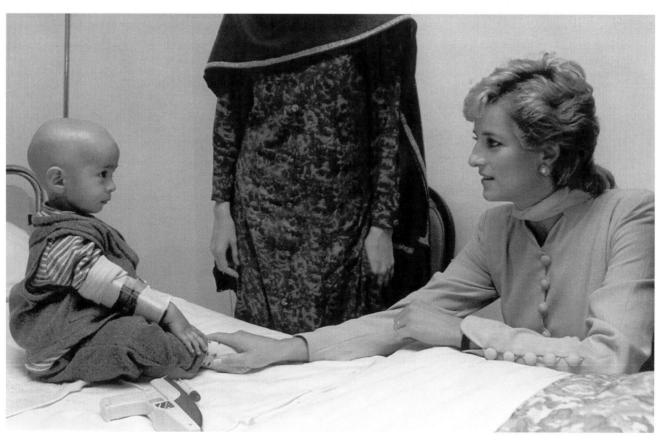

any carefree day with friends for that matter – the fortification of alcohol. After lunch she helped clear the table and stacked the dishwasher, soaked the pans and wiped the table with a damp cloth.

Then four of us went for a walk on Hampstead Heath. We were all arm-in-arm, plodding through mud after heavy rain in ordinary shoes, laughing at the state they were in. People passing us on the Heath could hardly believe they were seeing the most famous woman in the world entirely without her public make-up. She wore jeans and ankle boots. Her unstyled hair was its natural shape, flat.

But the simple soul who was the real Diana was already anticipating Christmas, which she hated because her sons inevitably spent it with their father and the rest of the Royal Family. She would be alone as usual, and told me she was going away to Barbuda for a few days. It was the solitary glum moment in a sunny afternoon, and she soon shrugged it off and began to have fun.

On that Saturday she didn't talk much about Dodi, and I understood why: she was afraid that the moment too much was read into the relationship it would end. She always feared that the pressures of publicity would alienate any man in her life. 'Who would have me with all the baggage I come with?' she would say.

She had told me she regretted admitting in her famous *Panorama* interview having an affair with James Hewitt, whom she had also loved.

So why had she said it? The answer was simplicity itself: Charles had admitted adultery on television, so why shouldn't she?

Whatever the psychiatrists said about her bulimia and its roots in her disrupted childhood, Diana believed that its main cause was the poor quality of her life with Charles – 'there were three of us in this marriage so it was a bit crowded,' as she told the *Panorama* audience.

This made her gloomy enough. And yet it never pushed her to the extremes of misery she felt when commentators and the public misunderstood what she was doing. Most of all, she hated being called 'manipulative' and privately railed against those who used the word to describe her. 'They don't even know me,' she would say bitterly, sitting cross-legged on the floor of her apartment in Kensington Palace and pouring tea from a china pot.

It was this blindness, as she saw it, to what she really was that led her seriously to consider living in another country where she hoped she would be understood.

The idea first emerged in her mind about three years before she died. 'I've got to find a place where I can have peace of mind,' she said to me. She considered France, because it was near enough to stay in close touch with William and Harry. She thought of America because she – naïvely, it must be said – saw it as a country so brimming over with glittery people and celebrities that she would be able to 'disappear'.

She also thought of South Africa, where her brother Charles has made his home, and even Australia because it was the furthest place she could think of from the seat of her unhappiness. But this would have separated her from her sons.

Everyone said she would go anywhere, do anything to have her picture taken, but in my view the truth was completely different. A good day for Diana was one where her picture was not taken and *paparazzi* photographers did not pursue her and clamber over her car.

'Why are they so obsessed with me?' she would ask me, and I tried to explain but never felt that she fully understood.

Millions of women dreamed of changing places with her, but the Princess that I knew yearned for the ordinary, humdrum routine of their lives.

'They don't know how lucky they are,' she would say.

On Saturday 30 August, just before Diana was joined by Dodi for that last fateful dinner at the Ritz in Paris, she told me how 'fed up' she was at being compared with Camilla.

'It's all so meaningless,' she said, and left it at that.

She didn't say, she never said, whether she thought Charles and Camilla should marry.

Then, knowing that as a journalist I often work at weekends, she said to me: 'Unplug your phone and get a good night's sleep.' They were her final words to me, uttered with the same warmth and consideration with which she wrote to my mother when my father died last December and then sent her tickets for the ballet I had told her my mother loved.

On that fateful Saturday evening, Diana was as happy as I have ever known her. For the first time in years, all was well with her world.

Chapter 1

A VERY REAL LOVE

Just a few weeks after her wedding, the new Princess of Wales wrote a letter of breathless happiness to her childhood nanny, Mary Clarke. 'I adore being married and having someone to devote my time to,' she wrote. Diana's letter was typically brief but Nanny Clarke was aware that the handful of lines penned by the girl she had looked after for so many years said much more.

She knew that Diana had finally got all she had ever wanted: happiness within a loving marriage.

Nanny Clarke should know. It was to her – after she was hired by the divorced Johnnie Spencer, Lord Althorp, to look after his four children at Park House, Sandringham, Norfolk, where the Royal Family were their neighbours – that the 9-year-old Diana memorably remarked: 'I never want to be divorced.'

The break-up of her parents' marriage left Diana with only one ambition: to fall in love, get married and have lots of children. And at the time of her poignant letter to Nanny Clarke, all that seemed to be attainable. After all,

the Princess reasoned with girlish logic, the marriage of the heir to the throne had to be permanent.

Why, hadn't Prince Charles made that very point seven years earlier while she was a 13-year-old still playing with her pony Romilly?

'In my position,' declared the then 26-year-old Charles, in words that must have haunted him later, 'obviously the last thing I could entertain is getting divorced'.

Imagine then how Diana had felt when, after they had been dating for seven months, the Prince of Wales telephoned from a skiing holiday in Klosters in early February 1981 to tell the 19-year-old that he had 'something to ask her'. A few days later at Windsor Castle she found herself alone in his company.

As she was to recall years later, Charles sat her down and began by saying: 'I've missed you so much.' He didn't take her hand – 'there was never anything tactile about him' – but then he said: 'Will you marry me?'

'I remember thinking: "This is a joke." And I said: "Yeah, OK," and laughed. He was deadly serious. He

(Above): Diana blushes as Prince Charles turns to kiss her at a polo match at Cirencester during the early years of their marriage. (Opposite): Charles was protective of the nervous Diana on their first public appearances together and would constantly reassure her.

said: "You do realize that one day you will be Queen."

'And a voice inside me said: "You won't be Queen but you'll have a tough role." So I thought OK, and said: "Yes… I love you so much, I love you so much." To which he said: "Whatever love means." He said it then! I thought that was great! I thought he meant that! And so he ran upstairs and rang his mother.'

Later, on the day of their engagement, the Prince, perhaps incautiously, repeated the phrase 'whatever love means' when the couple were being interviewed by the world's media.

He was to be much criticized for those words but it should be remembered that this is the man who took seven weighty volumes by Sir Laurens Van der Post on honeymoon and, as Diana later lamented, read aloud the thoughts of his South African philosopher guru to his bride.

Charles would often cut a single bloom and present it to Diana with a kiss.

As Diana described it: 'Second night, out come the Van der Post novels he hadn't read. Seven of them. They came on our honeymoon. He read them and we had to analyze them over lunch every day.'

So what did 'love' mean to Charles and Diana? The question is worth asking because the generally held perception, one encouraged by the bleak picture painted by Andrew Morton's books and the tragic events of later years, was that theirs was a rancorous, loveless union that was doomed from the start.

The truth is the opposite. We have talked to a wide range of people, many of whom have never spoken publicly before, who have confirmed that there were years – despite the ever-present shadow of Camilla Parker Bowles – when there was profound love and joy in the relationship. Indeed, many believe that with a degree more patience on each side, the marriage could have survived.

The Prince would often cut a rose from his beloved garden at Highgrove, his country home in Gloucestershire, and give Diana the single stem with a kiss.

Love was certainly in the air when the couple became engaged. Charles confided to close friends that while he did not yet love Diana, she was 'lovable and warm-hearted'. He was sure, he said, that he could 'fall in love with her'. She had no 'past'. No lovers to kiss and tell and, crucially, she had never been in love before.

The Prince took enormous pleasure in the belief that in marrying Diana, he would be both her first and, significantly, her last love. So we can assume that he went into marriage with a girl almost thirteen years his junior with the same expectation of permanence that he had expressed six years earlier.

But it was more than that. Diana's apparently uncomplicated sweetness and youthful enthusiasm tantalized him. The hints had been there for ages, ever since he had invited the 16-year-old Diana to show him the gallery at Althorp, the Spencer family's ancestral home in Northamptonshire, instead of her sister Lady Sarah – older by six years – whom he had been courting.

After Diana had agreed to become his wife, the Prince wrote to a friend: 'I do believe I am very lucky that someone as special as Diana seems to love me so much. I am already discovering how nice it is to have someone around to share things with.' Their love was to find a

*This charming picture taken when William was six months old shows,
in Diana's words: 'Charles loved the nursery life and couldn't wait to get back to it'.*

new intensity after the marriage. Diana would later tell friends that she and Charles had 'some truly wonderful times', especially in the years encompassing the births of William in 1982 and Harry two years later.

And their love deepened as Diana took great joy in teaching the repressed and innately anxious Prince how to be tactile with baby William. Charles was, it must be said, a man to whom cuddling and kissing did not come naturally, but his wife certainly changed all that.

They loved reading poetry together and listening to classical music, especially Tchaikovsky. Even in 1997, when her friend Simone Simmons gave her a collection of Tchaikovsky ballet music, Diana remarked that it so reminded her of Charles. Diana could identify any of the composer's symphonies from just a few notes. Thus, the record library of classical music wasn't *his*, and the pop collection *hers*, as popularly imagined, but *theirs*.

Diana described to Nanny Clarke how Charles 'loved the nursery life and couldn't wait to get back and do the bottle and everything. He was very good, he always came back and fed the baby.' (She breast-fed William for three weeks and Harry for eleven weeks.)

Charles was with Diana when William was born on 21 June 1982 – induced followed by a lengthy labour – and the Princess laughingly told a close friend: 'I was calling "Hold my hand, Charles, hold my hand," but he was much more interested in what was happening at the other end. Charles was too engrossed with what was going on in the front of the engine.'

The Prince wrote to his godmother Lady Patricia Brabourne, daughter of Earl Mountbatten: 'I am so thankful I was beside Diana's bedside the whole time because, by the end of the day, I really felt as though I'd shared deeply in the process of birth and as a result was

rewarded by seeing a small creature that belonged to *us* even though he seemed to belong to everyone else as well.'

The happiest time of their marriage, according to Diana, was the high summer of 1984 when she was expecting Harry: 'We were very, very close to each other... the closest we've ever, ever been and ever will be.'

She never got round to explaining just what this closeness was, but others remember the heavily pregnant Princess at Smith's Lawn polo ground at Windsor on her third wedding anniversary looking the picture of happiness as she clapped her husband onto the field. They were even pictured stealing a kiss behind a Land Rover in Windsor Great Park.

There were, however, already two dark shadows over their union: Camilla Parker Bowles and the bulimia that, as we shall see later, had its roots in the Princess's childhood.

It was on their honeymoon on board Britannia, that Diana's bulimia became serious. She would eat and then get sick, and suffer severe mood swings, from happiness to tears.

And yet the honeymoon was far from being all bad. As Diana was to recall of that time, Charles 'was blissfully happy, and as long as he was happy that was fine'.

Indeed, what emerges from our extensive conversations with so many people close to the pair is the effort both of them put into making the marriage work.

'But for Camilla...' was the phrase we heard over and over, usually followed by the view that it was the older

woman who should have made the decision to get out of their lives, not the Prince because, as we were repeatedly told, 'Charles is weak'.

Whether or not Charles had finished with Camilla as a mistress, as he insisted to Diana before the marriage, it was, in the view of Mary Clarke among several others, the 'other woman's' constant shadow that exacerbated the bulimia that did so much to undermine the marriage. It was this eating disorder – with which, in the Queen's view, her son simply could not cope – which apparently drove him back into the arms of Camilla. This made the bulimia even worse, and so the cycle of despair gathered pace.

One of Diana's closest confidantes, the wife of a prominent peer, told us it should have been plain from the earliest days of their marriage that both Diana and Charles needed special help, particularly when, during and immediately after her first pregnancy, the Princess began to suffer severe bouts of depression which the Royal Family and especially Charles 'simply didn't seem to understand'.

Charles never saw his mother show weakness. She always got on with the job in hand. Duty overrode everything. Not surprisingly, his attitude to Diana was: 'Pull yourself together, get on with things.'

'If only Diana had sought proper advice about her marriage from the right people instead of turning to that dreadful man Andrew Morton, things might have been different,' says Nanny Clarke, talking as never before about the Princess. 'Morton got her at her most vulnerable and has tried to fossilize her in that bleak period when she was unimaginably unhappy. She told me she bitterly regretted helping with that book. She said she wasn't her true self then but a desperate woman searching for a way out.

'In fact, re-reading her letters to me, it's clear she still hoped that somehow their marriage could be saved. They were always so warm and full of hopes and dreams, just as she was when she was a little girl.'

In 1997, Diana told the peer's wife she believed her

marriage could have been saved. 'You know, it didn't need to turn out the way it did,' she said.

For a long time after they separated in 1992, Diana kept Charles's sitting room at Kensington Palace just the same, so that if he suddenly walked back in everything would be as it had been on the day he left.

'It was partly for the boys, of course,' says her friend Simone Simmons. 'It broke her up one Christmas after the separation when she was talking to them about presents and they said what they really wanted was for her and Papa to get back together.'

In the garden at Kensington Palace on William's second birthday in June 1984.
Diana was six months pregnant with Harry. She later said that the weeks
before his birth were the happiest in the marriage.

Chapter 2

DESTINED TO BE DIFFERENT

Last thing at night, two small children, aged seven and four, knelt by their beds. It was 1968 and Diana Spencer and her little brother Charles were, as always, saying the Lord's Prayer followed by a personal prayer in which they blessed everyone they knew, especially Daddy and their absent mother.

At the weekend, as usual, they would be driven from Park House, their home at Sandringham, Norfolk, where Diana was born, to King's Lynn railway station.

There, with their nanny, they would board the train and at the end of the journey at London's Liverpool Street station they would be met by their anxious mother Frances, waiting for them at the barrier.

She was now Mrs Peter Shand Kydd, the wife of an urbane and good-looking businessman whom she had met some years earlier at a dinner party.

There was love for the children at both ends of the railway line, but also tension and unhappiness that was to

make unforgettable inroads into their young lives.

As the adult Diana was to recall: 'I remember Mummy crying an awful lot. When we went up for weekends, every Saturday night, standard procedure, she would start crying.

'We would both see her crying. We'd say: "What's the matter, Mummy?"

'She'd say: "Oh, I don't want you to leave tomorrow." Which for a nine-year-old was devastating, you know.'

The biggest disruption in Diana's childhood was not so much her parents' divorce in April 1969 when she was seven, but the separation eighteen months earlier when, as she put it a quarter of a century later (perhaps with a hint of understanding): 'Mummy decided to leg it.'

Inevitably, there have long been rumours of Earl Spencer's overbearing manner and bullying towards his first wife.

For her part, Diana recalled: 'We all have our own interpretations of what should have happened and what

(Opposite): *This favourite family picture was taken by Earl Spencer. After their parents' divorce, Diana and her younger brother Charles turned increasingly to each other for support.* (Above): *Johnnie and Frances Spencer at Diana's christening in 1961.*

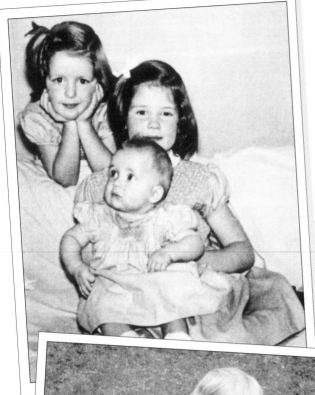

did happen. People took sides. Various people didn't speak to each other. For my brother and I it was a very wishy-washy and painful experience.'

It was not, perhaps, as upsetting for the older Spencer sisters, Sarah and Jane, who were at boarding school.

Until the arrival of Mary Clarke in 1970, nannies came and went with alarming regularity. The reason, as Diana explained, was that if she and Charles didn't like the latest arrival 'we used to stick pins in her chair and throw her clothes out of the window. We always thought nannies were a threat because they tried to take mother's position'.

Diana's consolation was to fill her bed with friends: she cuddled up to no fewer than twenty stuffed animals

(Top left): *Sarah, Jane and baby Diana.*
(Centre left): *Diana's first birthday.*
(Bottom left): *She loved to mother little Charles.*

(Above):
Johnnie Spencer surrounded by his children (from left) Sarah, Charles, Jane and, sitting apart, Diana.

(Left):
The 8-year-old Diana's dream of being a bridesmaid – squired by her pageboy brother Charles – was ruined by her agonising dilemma over a rehearsal dress.

at night. 'That was my family,' she said. They were still with her (though now on the sofa in her bedroom) during the last years of her life at Kensington Palace.

She needed them because she was afraid of the dark and had to have a light on outside her door until she was ten. 'I used to hear my brother crying in his bed down at the other end of the house, crying for my mother. He was unhappy, too.'

Diana would have gone and comforted him as she was to help so many people later in her life, but she could not 'pluck up the courage to get out of bed', especially as their father's room was in another part of the big house.

Holidays, Diana said, were 'always very grim. Two weeks with Mummy and two weeks with Daddy, and the trauma of going from one house to another, with each

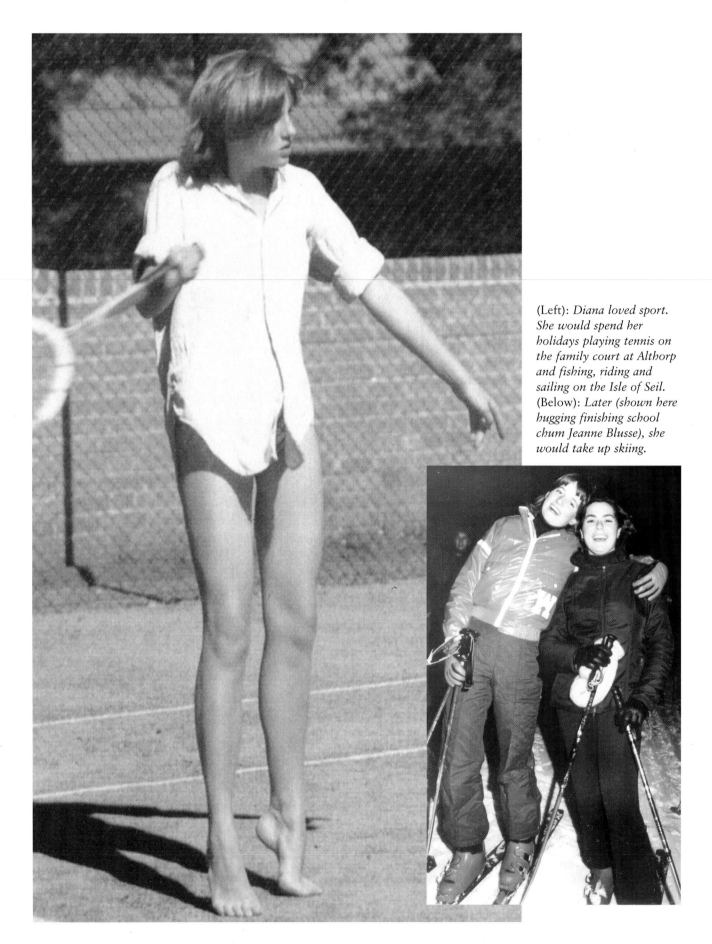

(Left): *Diana loved sport. She would spend her holidays playing tennis on the family court at Althorp and fishing, riding and sailing on the Isle of Seil.* (Below): *Later (shown here hugging finishing school chum Jeanne Blusse), she would take up skiing.*

parent trying to make it up with material things rather than the actual tactile stuff, which is what we both craved but neither of us ever got'.

Nothing more graphically illustrates Diana's recollection of her discomfort at the on-going war between her parents than her story of the bridesmaid's dress.

She was eight and was at last to realize her dream of being a bridesmaid. It was to be at the society wedding of her cousin Elizabeth Wake-Walker to Anthony Duckworth-Chad.

Diana arrived in London with a white dress her father had given her for the rehearsal to find her mother had a green frock for her to wear. She was torn between which one to choose. She later described it as 'the most agonising decision I ever had to make'. She finally chose the green dress because her mother was attending the rehearsal. (This recollection has baffled her mother who does not recall any conflict over dresses.)

Despite the traumas caused by her divided loyalties to her parents, there is much evidence that there was also considerable laughter and happiness throughout Diana's childhood.

Before her mother left Park House, it had been an idyllic place to grow up, surrounded by open country and only half a dozen miles from the Norfolk coast, where the family had a private beach hut at Brancaster.

Park House was noisy, filled with the homely sounds of children sliding down the banisters, playing hide-and-seek, and looking after pets. Diana had guinea pigs, hamsters, rabbits and a cat, Marmalade, which was hated by her brother Charles and sister Jane.

There was also, however, at Sandringham parish church the little grave of their infant brother John, the first-born son who had lived for just a few hours. As children, Diana and her brother Charles would often visit the grave.

Each had their own reason for this unusual fascination, though Charles would not come to realize until he was older that if John had survived, he would not have inherited the title and Althorp, the family's ancestral home in Northamptonshire.

Diana knew she was 'the girl who was supposed to be a boy', and this was to trouble her for much of her life though, in the end, she said she got used to it.

From a very young age, Diana felt rejected – because she was born a girl, by her mother's departure and by being sent to boarding school.

She described her parents, who already had two daughters when she was born on 1 July 1961, as being 'crazy to have a son and heir and then there comes a third daughter. What a bore, we're going to have to try again'.

No one knows for certain how young Diana was when she realized she was meant to be the boy who would carry on the 200-year-old earldom.

Her recollection was of recognizing feelings of rejection when she was very young. It was the first of four crucial times in her life that stirred such emotions.

The second was her mother's departure (although Frances did fight to take Diana and Charles with her). The third was her father leaving her on her first day at prep school. The fourth was caused by the Prince of Wales.

Was Diana right to feel rejected in those early years? The evidence is not conclusive. Her old nanny, Mary Clarke, praises the love and attention both parents gave their children, albeit under separate roofs.

Then again, the young Diana was extremely fond of her stepfather and, equally important, he of her.

Diana was ten when the Shand Kydds moved to a 1,000-acre farm on the Isle of Seil off the west coast of Scotland. She loved holidays with them, fishing, lobster-potting and riding her Shetland pony, Soufflé, which they kept there for her. Her stepfather, a former Navy submariner whose first wife had named Frances in her divorce action, taught her to sail.

It was the dashing and witty Peter Shand Kydd who gave Diana the nickname 'Duchess', shortened for the rest of her life by her family and close friends to 'Duch'.

No one is certain why he gave her that sobriquet, but a duchess is one step up the aristocratic ladder from a countess, the title her mother would have had if she had remained with Johnnie Spencer. And it was generally recognized that Diana was somehow 'different', almost elevated above the others because of the way she always maintained a 'private self'.

It was well-known in the family that Diana believed, even when she was very little, that she would grow up to marry someone important. She told them, especially after her parents parted, that she would marry a 'Prince Charming'. The phrase is, of course, chillingly, and coin-cidentally, close to Prince Charles.

As a child, Diana was not in awe of the Royal Family who spent several weeks a year in the large mansion she could see from her bedroom window at Sandringham. Quite naturally, the Spencer children got to know its younger members, Andrew and Edward, though they never became close friends. On one occasion, Diana rebelled against going to one of the royal children's parties because she refused to endure the boredom of seeing the film *Chitty Chitty Bang Bang* for the third successive year. Apparently, the Queen always showed it.

(Left): *Diana swam as often as she could in the family swimming pool at Althorp;* (Opposite top): *the Spencer children soon had their own cars;* (Opposite right): *after leaving school, Diana spent a term improving her skiing at a Swiss finishing school;* (Far right): *Diana with her mother, Frances Shand Kydd.*

The idealistic teenager, reading a romantic novel by her step-grandmother, Barbara Cartland.

It has been suggested – and quite cruelly reinforced by the repeated anecdote of Diana wondering aloud if she would be 'fortunate enough' to marry Charles – that from an early age she set her cap at the most prestigious union it was possible to make.

The truth is that while her father was excited by the notion of any of his daughters marrying into the unique neighbours his family had served for generations, Diana had no particular man or dynasty in mind. As she was to say: 'I always felt different from everyone else, very detached. I knew I was going somewhere different but had no idea where.

'I said to my father when I was thirteen: "I know I'm going to marry someone in the public eye." I was thinking more of being an ambassador's wife – not the top one [the Prince of Wales].'

Indeed, the young Lady Diana never gave Charles a thought until he started to pursue her. Even her father, a former equerry to both George VI and the Queen, who always hoped at least one of his daughters would marry a Prince, hadn't considered it. Charles was, after all, almost thirteen years older than Diana.

Then one Sunday morning, the family returned from church where they had seen the Royal Family at prayer, and the 11-year-old Diana casually remarked that she thought Prince Andrew was 'very good-looking'.

It delighted her father because he had privately earmarked Andrew, just a year older than Diana, as the most likely royal suitor (if there were to be one) for his youngest daughter. Her sisters took a devilish pleasure in

never allowing her to forget this admission, pulling her leg mercilessly about her having a crush on Andrew. She would turn scarlet and say it was rubbish.

By that time she was at Riddlesworth Hall, the prep school she had been attending from the age of eight. (Her early hopes of joining a ballet school had been dashed, as her teachers had told her that it was an impossible dream because she was growing so tall). This didn't diminish her love of performing, though she glumly admitted to her sisters that she believed she danced 'like an elephant'.

When her father deposited her on her first day at the school, a two-hour drive from home, Diana's initial feelings were of rejection.

'I used to make threats such as "If you love me you won't leave me here", which was jolly unkind to him,' she recalled. 'Actually, I loved being at school.'

She represented her house, Nightingale, at netball and swimming, and was popular with the other girls. A friend at Riddlesworth was Harriet Bowden, who is now a stand-up comedienne in London. She liked Diana because 'she was into breaking the rules'.

On one occasion, the pair went for a midnight walk in their pyjamas down the school drive.

Their absence from the dormitory brought all the staff out with torches, frantically trying to find them. Harriet was quickly caught but Diana managed to evade capture for much longer.

When, aged twelve, Diana joined her sisters at West Heath School in Kent, she shared a dormitory with Sarah Edwards, who is now married to an accountant.

They giggled over Mills and Boon love stories after lights out and got up to mischief. They would pinch chocolate biscuits and margarine and melt them together on a radiator to make cakes – this from a soon-to-be Princess whose life would be wrecked by bulimia.

Diana was also keen on domestic pleasures, and she and Sarah used to go to meals early because they liked helping to set the tables.

This was very much the same Diana – enjoying simple pursuits, laughing at silly things and dreaming of love – whom the Prince of Wales courted to the point where he wanted to marry her.

*Dressed in all her finery, the 18-year-old Diana leafs
through a magazine before a grand ball at Althorp.*

Chapter 3

A GIRL
WHO 'KEPT
HERSELF TIDY'

For a boy of 16, it was an unexpected bonus to be singled out by an older girl who danced with him, and only him, all night long. The boy was Sholto Douglas-Home, the occasion his birthday party at a village hall in Norfolk, and the girl who claimed him was his 17-year-old cousin, Lady Diana Spencer.

'She just seemed to find it easier dancing with someone who was a relative,' says Sholto, whose mother is the former model Sandra Paul, now married to Shadow Foreign Secretary Michael Howard.

But there was a very good reason why Diana stayed close to her family that night. She had made a private decision not to get involved romantically until she had met the 'Prince Charming' she believed it was her destiny to

marry. As she explained years later: 'All my friends had boyfriends but not me, because I knew somehow that I had to keep myself very tidy for whatever was coming my way.'

It is a quaint expression, keeping herself 'tidy', used mainly in upper-class and aristocratic circles. What it means is remaining a virgin. And at the time of that party, as Sholto (now thirty-five and British Telecom's head of advertising) twirled her about to the disco music, she had already met the Prince of Wales and was aware that he liked her.

Nothing more at that stage, but he had stirred something in Diana. What was it? From childhood and the departure of her mother, she had felt a need to 'mother', beginning with her little brother Charles.

(Opposite): *The first photograph of Diana after the news broke of her relationship with the Prince in late 1980. It was taken at the Young England Kindergarten, where she was working.*
(Above): *In what is believed to be the first picture of Charles and Diana together, the couple watch the action during a shoot on the Althorp estate.*

Diana was sixteen in 1977 when she met the Prince of Wales for the first time. He had been invited to a shoot at Althorp by his then girlfriend, Diana's eldest sister Sarah, and arrived with his labrador.

Diana's first impression was: 'What a sad man.' She tried to cheer him up.

She remembered her sister being 'all over him like a bad rash' – one of her favourite expressions – while she herself mostly 'kept out of the way'. Her recollection of herself at that time was of being 'a fat, podgy, no-make-up, unsmart lady, but I made a lot of noise and he liked that'.

In fact, that evening at dinner, Pendrey the butler noticed the Prince's reaction to Diana, who was wearing a ballgown. He told his wife Maudie, the housekeeper, that Charles had 'taken a shine' to the teenager. Later, Diana confided in him that she thought the Prince was 'very nice'.

Charles saw in Diana a 'jolly and bouncy', unaffected and irreverent teenager, who was relaxed and friendly. Charles, of course, was looking for a special kind of bride and was soon to come under pressure, especially from Prince Philip, to get on with it.

Two months after Sholto's birthday party, the 'tidy' Diana was invited to celebrate Prince Charles's 30th birthday at Buckingham Palace.

The Prince's romance with her sister had cooled. His companion that November evening was the actress Susan George, pert, blonde and sexy but never a contender in the royal marriage stakes.

Diana had just returned after three unhappy months at a hated Swiss finishing school, and was about to start work as a nanny in Hampshire for Major Jeremy Whitaker and his wife Philippa, looking after their small daughter Alexandra.

From there, she went to work at the Young England Kindergarten in Pimlico, London, and two afternoons a week she looked after Patrick Robinson, the infant son of an American oil executive. The future Princess of Wales was also being paid £1 an hour to clean the Chelsea flat which her sister Sarah shared with theatre producer Lucinda Craig Harvey. (When they met some years afterwards and Lucinda dropped a curtsy, the Princess laughingly exclaimed: 'I should be curtsying to you, Lucinda – you used to be my employer.')

So Diana was intrigued to find herself at the Buckingham Palace birthday party, later observing that 'I had a very nice time at the dance – fascinating. I wasn't at all intimidated by the surroundings. I thought: "What an amazing place" '.

She wasn't what one would call aware, socially, at all,' says Lady Abel Smith, who is godmother to Diana's oldest sister Sarah and a lady-in-waiting to the Queen.

'She was pretty and there was a certain something about her, but she was quite shy and didn't really get involved with the social set. She had no social life to speak of before she became engaged.'

Living in a bachelor-girl flat in Earl's Court, Diana's life was not entirely without male relationships, but she kept them casual even though they – as one of them, Guards officer Rory Scott, has said – found her 'very sexually attractive'. As he confessed: 'The relationship was not a platonic one as far as I was concerned, but it remained that way.'

Another boyfriend, Adam Russell (great grandson of Prime Minister Stanley Baldwin and now a farmer in Dorset) went away to travel for a year hoping to renew his friendship with Diana on his return. But when he got back, he was greeted with the news that he had a rival: the Prince of Wales.

So it was that one July evening in 1980, the Prince, four months short of his 32nd birthday, found himself sitting on a hay bale at a barbecue in the grounds of the country home in Petworth, West Sussex, of the Queen's friends Commander Robert and Philippa de Pass. Lady Diana Spencer, only just nineteen, was beside him.

Since Charles's 30th birthday party, there had been casual meetings between the two, usually at shooting parties in Norfolk. But nothing more. Charles, in fact, had only just finished dating Anna Wallace, the pretty daughter of a Scottish landowner.

It was Glorious Goodwood week and Diana had been invited for the weekend by the de Pass's son Philip, who told her: 'We've got the Prince of Wales staying. You're a young blood, you might amuse him.'

In the afternoon, Diana had watched Charles play polo at nearby Cowdray Park and now, as the dozen guests drifted round the barbecue in the early summer evening, they talked.

Even at one of her very first public appearances, Diana had discovered her remarkable rapport with the camera.

Perhaps unwittingly, she struck a deep emotional chord in him by talking about the murder of his great-uncle and counsellor Earl Mountbatten, blown up by the IRA in a fishing boat in Ireland the previous August.

She said to Charles: 'You looked so sad when you walked up the aisle at Lord Mountbatten's funeral. It was the most tragic thing I've ever seen. My heart bled for you when I watched. I thought: "It's wrong, you're lonely, you should be with someone who would look after you."'

The Prince found himself moved by such compassion from a young girl. They talked on and it was not long before, in Diana's recollection, Charles was 'all over me... I thought this isn't very cool... I thought men were not supposed to be so obvious. He practically leapt on me and I thought this was very strange. I wasn't quite sure how to cope with all this... frigid wasn't the word.'

So taken was he by her that the Prince immediately invited Diana to return with him to Buckingham Palace. Uncertain about what to do, but knowing it would be improper to leave the house party, she declined.

Neither the de Pass family nor any of their other guests had noticed anything special happening between the Prince and the teenager. But if Diana did have a moment of destiny, then this encounter on the hay bale was it. Within days, Charles was telling his closest friends that he had met the girl he intended to marry.

The following month he invited Diana to join his party aboard Britannia for Cowes Week. While he wind-surfed, she went water-skiing.

She remembered him having 'lots of older friends there and I was fairly intimidated but they were all over me like a bad rash'.

The next, inevitable step was for the Prince to invite Diana to Balmoral, for the weekend of the Royal Braemar Gathering. Significantly, the Queen was there and the excuse used for Diana to join the house party without attracting premature attention was for her to stay with her sister Jane and her husband Robert Fellowes

Diana and Camilla mirror each other's body language as they watch Charles, riding as an amateur, come second at Ludlow Races in 1980. The teenager was beginning to wonder about the older woman's role in his life.

– then the Queen's assistant private secretary – at their cottage on the royal estate.

'I was terrified – sh***ing bricks. I was frightened because I had never stayed at Balmoral and I wanted to get it right,' Diana recalled. 'I was all right once I got in through the front door.'

Among the house party guests were Charles's great friends, Andrew and Camilla Parker Bowles, and Diana was soon to start wondering why 'they were there at all my visits'.

Charles for his part was growing increasingly attached to the tomboyish and seemingly uncomplicated teenager and her peals of laughter. One of his close friends and confidantes, Patty Palmer-Tomkinson, raved about Diana after they went stalking together.

'We got hot, we got tired, she fell into a bog, got covered in mud, laughed her head off, and got puce in the face with her hair glued to her forehead because it was pouring with rain.

'She was the sort of wonderful English schoolgirl who was game for anything, naturally young but sweet, and clearly determined and enthusiastic about him. She very much wanted him.'

Other friends took the view that Diana and Charles were too different for marriage to work and that Diana appeared unaware of the enormity of the role she was taking on. But the Prince wouldn't listen and got angry when his friend Lord Romsey, Earl Mountbatten's grandson, tried to raise such issues with him.

At that stage, Charles saw Diana in precisely the light that Mountbatten had suggested – a pure young girl with no past who could be moulded to fit the role of Princess of Wales.

For their part, the couple's maternal grandmothers, long-time best friends, the Queen Mother and Ruth, Lady Fermoy, were putting their heads together and deciding that Diana was right for Charles.

Lady Fermoy's apparent two-faced attitude to the union has caused considerable confusion since she has been unfairly portrayed as a woman saying one thing to the Royal Family and another to her own.

Charles lends a helping hand (left) as *Diana nervously faces the cameras during an early visit to Tetbury, near Highgrove, the Prince's country home* (top).

In fact her position was very clear. She did have doubts: not that Diana wasn't right for Charles but that Charles might not be right for Diana.

As Diana recalled, she was warned by her grandmother: 'Darling, you must understand that their sense of humour and lifestyle are different, and I don't think it will suit you.'

That said, when the Prince took Diana to the Albert Hall one Sunday for a performance of Verdi's Requiem – a favourite of hers – Lady Fermoy chaperoned her granddaughter back to Buckingham Palace for a cold supper in Charles's rooms.

Not long after this, Diana was being whisked down the M4 to spend the weekend at Bolehyde Manor in Wiltshire, home of Charles's friends, the Parker Bowleses. By October 1980, Diana was deeply in love with the Prince but she was already beginning to wonder about Camilla's role in his life.

She was repeatedly being surprised by how much Camilla knew of the relationship and even of what she and the Prince had talked about. When Charles took Diana to see his new home, Highgrove, she was alarmed to discover it was just eleven miles from Bolehyde.

But in those heady months it scarcely mattered. Diana was in love with this intriguing man who, though she still called him 'Sir', appeared to be so engagingly in need of being looked after.

By then, Charles had made up his mind to ask her to marry him, but Diana instinctively knew there was 'somebody else around' and that this someone was Camilla.

'I couldn't understand why she [Camilla] kept saying to me: "Don't push him into doing this, don't do that". She knew so much about what he was doing privately and about what we were doing privately... I couldn't understand it,' she said.

Diana's friends and sisters knew of her uncertainty, but she was being swept along by a combination of forces. There was her feeling of destiny and her conviction that ultimately she could overcome whatever attachment Charles had to another woman. But most of all she loved him.

Shortly before her wedding, a strained Diana, losing weight and lost in thought, leans against a car for support during a polo match.

*A glamorous Camilla out on the town around the time
that Charles had started to woo Diana.*

Chapter 4

DIANA AND HER FAMILY

The proudest moment of the 8th Earl Spencer's life was seeing his daughter Diana marry the heir to the throne. The worst was the Waleses's estrangement. Diana's achievement, as he saw it, was the apex of his personal ambition. His dismay when the marriage foundered was profound; he took it personally.

Too late he saw how wrong had been his ambition that his children should marry into the Royal Family. Of his daughters Sarah, Jane and Diana (whom he called the Three Graces), only the youngest fulfilled this dream. The worst thing for Diana, and therefore for himself, he told a friend, was her marrying a Royal.

Diana was perhaps closer to her father than his other three children because she most reminded him of Frances, the wife he had loved but lost when she had left him for another man. The Earl's death in 1992 hit Diana very hard because her marriage was in tatters and her father had been one of the few people who, with his

years as an equerry to George VI and the present Queen, fully understood the pressures she was under.

The only thing that had come between them had been his marriage to the Countess of Dartmouth in 1977. The first time he brought the impeccably coiffured Raine to lunch with his four children, he sent Sarah, the eldest daughter, to her room for deliberately burping. Diana defended her sister.

When she was fifteen, a year before her father remarried, Diana got a schoolfriend to write a poison pen letter to her future stepmother. And, together with her brother Charles, she told their father that if he married Raine 'we will wash our hands of you'. They didn't, of course.

Diana couldn't bring herself to break with the father who had brought her up. She also came to realize that Raine was good for him, recognizing that she had virtually resurrected him from near death after his stroke in 1978. Nevertheless, her resentment against the woman who had taken her mother's place simmered on. In 1989,

(Opposite): *Diana was a bridesmaid when Jane married Robert Fellowes in April 1978. Sadly, the sisters were to fall out.* (Above): *The teenage Diana had a strained relationship with her stepmother Raine, but she later came to admire her.*

The Three Graces, as their father called them (above, left to right) *Sarah, Diana and Jane, enjoy a night on the town together in November 1995.*

during a rehearsal for her brother Charles's wedding to the model Victoria Lockwood, the Princess had a blazing row with her stepmother because Raine refused to speak to Diana's mother, Frances Shand Kydd, who was sitting in the same pew.

Significantly, it was only after her father died that the Princess and Raine (whose belongings had been summarily shipped out of Althorp in black bin liners by the family) became friends.

Suddenly, the two women were seen lunching together. The Princess found wisdom and strength in the woman who had once been her bitter enemy. She also realized how much Raine had loved her father.

Somewhat to the disappointment of Diana's brother and sisters, their meetings became frequent and even warm. The Princess and her stepmother lunched at the Connaught, Diana's apartment in Kensington Palace and, after Raine became a non-executive director of Harrods, in Mohamed Al Fayed's boardroom.

The saddest part of the Spencer family story is what happened between Diana and Jane, the middle sister.

Jane was the steady one and the most academic. She was reliable, studious and sporty. In Diana's words, she was 'wonderfully solid. If you rang up with a drama, she'd say "Golly, gosh, Duch, how horrible, how sad and how awful" and get angry.'

When Diana became Princess of Wales, Jane was the most frequent family visitor at Highgrove, the Waleses's country home. The sisters were neighbours at Kensington Palace and saw a lot of each other because Jane had married into the Palace system, too: her husband, Sir Robert Fellowes, is the Queen's private secretary.

On the one hand, it helped her understand Diana's marital problems. On the other, it split Jane's loyalties, especially after Diana denied any involvement in the Morton book, a claim Sir Robert knew wasn't true.

Diana and Jane's sisterly friendship was one of the casualties of the bitter matrimonial struggle between Charles and Diana which became known as the War of the Waleses. They tried to cling on to what was left of their relationship but, tragically, for at least a year before the Princess's death, she and Jane rarely spoke.

In stark contrast, Diana's difficult relationship with her stepmother Raine mellowed in recent years as the two women found that they shared much in common.

Despite the problems with Jane, Diana always knew she could turn to her family for support. From childhood, she had idolized Sarah, now forty-two, the eldest of the four Spencer children.

Where Diana was afraid of horses after a childhood fall, Sarah was a fearless horsewoman. Where Diana tinkered timorously with the grand piano, Sarah was an accomplished performer. Where Diana always kept something in reserve, Sarah was exhilarating company, positive, organized and self-assured.

Diana so admired her red-haired sister that she could hardly believe it when Charles, who had courted Sarah for more than a year, switched his affections to her.

Sarah, now married to farmer Neil McCorquodale, felt nothing but relief when the prospect that she might marry into royalty had passed. It was no surprise that during the lowest years of Diana's marriage, her oldest sister became one of the people on whom she most depended.

Just before her separation from Charles in December 1992, Diana made Sarah her lady-in-waiting, explaining: 'She's the one person I know I can always trust.'

Sarah shared with Diana not only a courtship with Charles but the experience of going through an eating disorder. In her case, anorexia; in Diana's, bulimia.

Her response to criticisms that Diana should not have let the world know of her unhappy marriage through the Morton biography was to mount a swashbuckling defence. 'Well, she's still Duch and our sister and that's enough for me,' she would say. And Sarah made no secret of the fact that she considered that Charles 'did not do enough to take care of Duch'.

And finally, what about Diana's relationship with her brother Charles? To fully understand his breaking voice and aggressive indignation at her funeral, we must go back to tiny Silfield School in Gayton, King's Lynn.

(Above): *The Princess with Sarah, her ever supportive sister and lady-in-waiting, during a visit to New York in December 1996.*

(Left): *Diana and her little brother Charles play on the swing at Park House. The special bond between them was forged when they turned to each other for support after their parents separated.*

This was not, in fact, Diana's first school. She had previously been enrolled at the Francis Holland School in West London for the autumn term of 1967 when her mother, Frances, ran off with businessman Peter Shand Kydd taking Diana and Charles with her (Charles was enrolled at the Young England Kindergarten in Pimlico where Diana would later work).

When the two children went back to Norfolk for Christmas, their father did not allow them to return to their mother.

In the January, he enrolled them at Silfield, which still has the rocking horse on which Diana used to play with her brother. The swing on which she pushed him still dangles from the walnut tree in the school garden.

As the headmistress Evelyn Phillips told us, Diana was 'an excellent little mother to her brother Charles. She always looked after him'. This motherly instinct was seen as quite natural by Jean Lowe, the then headmistress of the friendly little school. For out of the school's sixty-five children, the Spencers were the only ones whose parents were separated. It was probably this experience that made Diana feel 'different' from others for the rest of her life.

During the difficult middle years of Diana's marriage, her brother Charles gave unstinting loyalty and backing

A rare family picture of the Prince and Princess of Wales with her older sisters Jane and Sarah and her younger brother Charles at his 21st birthday party in May 1985.

to the sister who had mothered him. Yet after her separation in December 1992, the Princess felt let down when her brother withdrew an offer to provide her with a cottage at Althorp, which he had inherited a year earlier.

Charles said he was concerned about security but he also knew that Diana's arrival would bring another unwelcome intrusion: the media, which he loathed.

Diana was very upset. She had gone as far as choosing wallpaper and fabrics for the four-bedroom Garden House that was to have been her bolt hole.

Once again in her life, Diana felt rejection. Her friends were angry with her brother but others understood his quandary. Even the Princess did so eventually and in March 1997 visited him at his new home in Cape Town.

So it was not surprising that at Diana's funeral service, her brother made such a swingeing attack on the media which had pursued the Princess and on the Royal Family who had shunned her. As he saw it, he and his sister had always been victims, and still were.

Chapter 5

THE STUFF OF FAIRYTALES

When a girl says 'Yes' to a proposal of marriage, she is bound to be flooded with emotions. These can range from doubts to exhilaration. Lady Diana Spencer felt pure joy. She believed Prince Charles was as much in love with her as she was with him. Why would he want her if that were not the case?

Diana painted a graphic word picture of girlish excitement on her return on the evening of Charles's proposal in early February 1981 to the Chelsea flat she now shared with three friends: 'I said: "Guess what?" They said: "He asked you? What did you say?" I replied: "Yes, please." Everybody screamed and howled. I rang my parents the next morning. Daddy was thrilled: "How wonderful." Mummy was thrilled. I told my brother and he said: "Who to?" '

The Prince, meanwhile, was also ringing round. He called his mother at Sandringham and then Diana's father, Earl Spencer, whom he asked: 'Can I marry your daughter? I have asked her and very surprisingly she said: "Yes." ' Lord Spencer replied: 'Well done.'

Later, when Diana came to see her father and told him she wanted to marry Prince Charles, he sat his daughter down. 'I told her she must marry the man she loves,' the late Johnnie Spencer said. 'Diana replied: "That is what I am doing."'

So what was Charles really thinking when Diana agreed to marry him? A few days later he wrote to a friend: 'Other people's happiness and enthusiasm at the whole thing is a most encouraging element and it makes me so proud that so many people have such admiration and affection for Diana.'

He described his engagement as 'la grande plonge'. Diana didn't put a handle on her happiness.

But it wasn't long before the first disappointment struck. Two days after his proposal, Diana flew to Australia with her mother Frances and stepfather Peter Shand Kydd for a three-week holiday in which to plan the wedding. Their address and telephone number were secret because of the intense media interest. Only one man knew where Diana was – the Prince of Wales.

(Above and opposite): *After the service, the Prince of Wales leads his new bride up the aisle to greet the adoring public outside.*

43

The Prince introduces his fiancée to the world with the official engagement picture taken on 24 February 1981.

Day after day, she waited for him to call. 'I pined for him,' she said, 'but he never rang. I thought that was very strange. Whenever I rang him, he was out and he never rang me back.'

When she got back from Australia, someone from Charles's office arrived with a bunch of flowers. As Diana said: 'I knew they hadn't come from Charles because there was no note. It was just somebody in the office being tactful.'

On the evening of 23 February, the day before the formal announcement and the official photo call at Buckingham Palace, Diana left her Chelsea flat for the last time and moved into Clarence House, the Queen Mother's home.

A letter lay on her bed. It was from Camilla Parker Bowles and said: 'Such exciting news about the engagement. Do let's have lunch soon when the Prince of Wales goes to Australia and New Zealand. He's going away for three weeks. I'd love to see the ring. Lots of love, Camilla.'

On the day of Charles's departure, Diana was famously photographed red-eyed and weepy at the airport. It was generally assumed that her tears were for the departing Prince. In reality, she was weeping because earlier that day she'd had to leave his study when a phone call came through from Camilla.

Despite this setback, Diana agreed to the lunch date. When Camilla asked if she was going to hunt when she lived at Highgrove, Prince Charles's country home, Diana replied that she wasn't. The older woman said:

'I just wanted to know.' Camilla and Charles, of course, both hunted with the Beaufort, as they still do, though these days never together.

Meanwhile, the engagement ring had to be decided upon, but choosing it was very different from the way most couples do things. The stones arrived in a briefcase and, although Diana made the final choice, most of the Royals had a say.

The central sapphire surrounded by diamonds was copied by brides all over the world. According to Diana, Charles didn't pay for it; the Queen did. Diana was feeling increasingly isolated in this new royal world: she had to feel her way instead of being tutored, as she had expected.

When, after a few days with the Queen Mother at Clarence House, she was moved into a suite of rooms in Buckingham Palace, even Prince Charles recognized that it must have seemed remote and inhospitable to his future bride.

But little advice was offered and, with singularly bad timing, Diana's arrival at the Palace coincided with the three-week official trip to Australia and New Zealand which Charles 'much regretted' having to make.

Diana was lonely. 'I missed my girls (her flatmates) so much. I wanted to go back there and sit and giggle like we used to and borrow each other's clothes and chat about silly things, just being in my safe shell again.'

As her flatmate Carolyn Bartholomew saw it: 'She went to live at Buckingham Palace and then the tears started. This little thing got so thin. I was so worried about her.

'She wasn't happy, she was suddenly plunged into all this pressure and it was a nightmare for her. She was dizzy with it, bombarded from all sides. It was a whirlwind and she was ashen, she was grey.' But Diana's shrinking condition was not just because of her bewilderment. She was also afraid – especially after the puzzling unspoken messages of that lunch with Camilla – that she was marrying a man who might be involved with someone else.

Significantly, it was at about this time, quite early in the engagement, that the eating disorder bulimia started. When Diana, who was by then achieving celebrity status, was asked what she had for breakfast, she laughingly replied that she did not have anything. Nobody picked up the point.

EBY 776J

Diana chatting with Sarah Ferguson three days before the wedding

As Diana walked down the aisle on her father's arm, she spotted Camilla's face in the congregation.

Nor would anyone guess that when Charles put his arm around his fiancée's 29in waist and remarked that she was 'a bit chubby', it would have shrunk to 23in by her wedding day just five months later.

And there was the first evidence of her mood swings. The picture on the left, taken at a polo match just three days before the wedding, shows an excited Diana chatting to her friend Sarah Ferguson about her plans. Yet in the same week she had been seen publicly in tears.

Two weeks before the wedding, Charles had sent a memo to a member of staff asking for a bracelet to be ordered as a gift. He instructed that it be inscribed with the initials 'GF'. Some in the office believed this stood for 'Girl Friday'; others thought it meant 'Gladys and Fred', Charles and Camilla's goon-style pet names for each other.

Somehow, the bracelet ended up among the wedding gifts flooding in from all over the world. Diana wandered into the office and, thinking the package was a wedding gift, opened it. She rushed out in tears.

As Charles was privately giving the bracelet to Mrs Parker Bowles as a 'farewell' present two days before the wedding, Diana was pouring out her fears to her sisters over lunch in her rooms at Buckingham Palace.

She told them that Camilla's presence had been disturbing her to the point where she wondered whether she should go through with the marriage. Sarah and Jane tried to jolly her out of her fears, which they believed were natural pre-marriage nerves.

Jokingly, they said to their little sister: 'Bad luck, Duch. Your face is on the tea towels, so it's too late to chicken out.'

Every bride is entitled to a faultless wedding day, devoting her energies to nothing except looking beautiful. But as Lady Diana Spencer walked down the aisle on the arm of her father at St Paul's Cathedral on 29 July 1981, something else was on her mind, and her blue eyes were darting left and right.

Eventually, as she neared the end of the 625ft aisle that had taken three-and-a-half minutes to walk with the frail Earl Spencer to the resounding notes of Jeremiah Clarke's Trumpet Voluntary, Diana caught sight of what she was looking for.

There, three rows back on the left side, was the pale grey pillbox hat that Camilla Parker Bowles had said she would be wearing to the wedding. To Diana's right at that spot were Denis and Margaret Thatcher, and the Prime Minister's confidant, Willie Whitelaw.

Princess Grace of Monaco (who had famously joked with Diana in the ladies' room at Goldsmith's Hall in London on the teenager's first public engagement: 'Don't worry, it will get a lot worse') was among the congregation. So was Nancy Reagan, President and Mme Mitterrand of France... there were 21 sovereigns, 20 heads of state, 26 governors general, all focusing on the bride. But Diana's focus was on Camilla, whose 7-year-old son Tom, one of Prince Charles's godsons, was standing on his chair.

At this moment during the most glittering wedding the world had ever seen – and much of the globe was watching on television – this image of Camilla's pillbox hat was the one that Diana would always carry with her. A decade later, she would still be saying: 'To this day, you know – vivid memory.'

Her bridal dream that brilliant summer day was that this would be the last she would see of Mrs Parker Bowles in the Prince's life. She told herself: 'Let's hope that's all over with.' Outside the great cathedral, it almost looked as though it was. A million people were on the streets of London willing this decorative addition to the Royal Family to be happy. Many had been there all night, staking out their places. Right from the start, the people loved her.

Diana had spent her last unmarried night at Clarence House, the Queen Mother's home. Then, helped by the couturiers David and Elizabeth Emanuel, she stepped into her stunning wedding dress of ivory silk, with its 25ft train. The Spencer family diamond tiara and a tulle veil were put in place.

At 10.35am, her father arrived to collect her and she stepped into the royal Glass Coach whose other bridal

That famous kiss on the Buckingham Palace balcony.

occupants this century have included both the Queen and the Queen Mother.

The journey to St Paul's was a wall of cheers, a tidal outpouring of emotion that would not be matched, albeit in a very different form, until Diana's death 16 years later.

Lord Spencer was moved almost to tears by the adulation that swept along the route and continued as Diana finally stepped out onto the red carpet at the foot of the cathedral steps.

Bunched up in the coach, the long train had creased badly. Princess Margaret's daughter Lady Sarah Armstrong-Jones and Earl Mountbatten's granddaughter India Hicks smoothed it out and straightened it before the bride and her father began the slow climb up the granite steps to the cathedral door.

Everyone was worried about Lord Spencer because he was recovering from a stroke. He had come back from near death, helped by his second wife Raine, the former Countess of Dartmouth.

No one worried about the bride. Why should they? She was radiant and happy – after all, she was marrying the most eligible man in the land.

Little did the crowds know that, as we have described, but for her sisters calming her anxieties about Camilla, this most spectacular of royal weddings could even have been called off.

But something else had also soothed Diana and brought her to St Paul's. It was the arrival on her wedding eve of a special delivery from Charles.

On black velvet inside a jeweller's box lay a signet ring engraved with the Prince of Wales feathers, and a card which said: 'I'm so proud of you and when you come up I'll be there at the altar for you tomorrow. Just look 'em in the eye and knock 'em dead.'

Now it was happening. Diana carried a bouquet of stephanotis, white orchids and lilies of the valley, with gold roses in memory of Lord Mountbatten and a sprig of myrtle cut from a bush grown from a spray in Queen Victoria's wedding bouquet in 1840.

The Archbishop of Canterbury, Robert Runcie, had agonized over his address and rewritten it several times. He was not helped by the feeling that he was officiating at an arranged marriage, but his view was: 'They're a nice couple and she'll grow into it.'

And so he began with the oft-quoted words: 'Here is the stuff of which fairy tales are made...'

Not quoted quite so often are his words of caution: 'Those who are married live happily ever after the wedding day if they persevere in the real adventure which is the royal task of creating each other and creating a more loving world.'

The show went on all day in the streets outside as an estimated 750 million watched on television round the world.

Diana's recollection of the crowds which filled The Mall for that famous kiss on the balcony of Buckingham Palace was 'overwhelming... so humbling, all these thousands and thousands of happy people. It was just wonderful'.

Writing some days later to a friend, Prince Charles said: 'What an unbelievable day it was – that went far too quickly. I couldn't somehow savour all I wanted to savour.

'I was totally overwhelmed and overcome by the way in which the whole country seemed to have been a favourite guest at the wedding.'

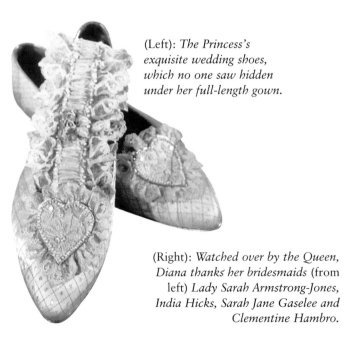

(Left): *The Princess's exquisite wedding shoes, which no one saw hidden under her full-length gown.*

(Right): *Watched over by the Queen, Diana thanks her bridesmaids (from left)* Lady Sarah Armstrong-Jones, India Hicks, Sarah Jane Gaselee and Clementine Hambro.

Chapter 5

THE HONEYMOON IS OVER

As he packed the Prince of Wales's honeymoon luggage at Buckingham Palace, valet Stephen Barry ticked off the items on a check list. Fishing rods, seven novels by Sir Laurens Van der Post, brushes and easel, cuff links. All would play their part in the honeymoon, especially the cuff links...

Like all brides, Princess Diana would come home with many beautiful memories of those first weeks of married life. But she also came home with some doubts.

In the eyes of the world, Charles and Diana were the luckiest couple on earth. First, they spent three days at the Hampshire home of the late Lord Mountbatten to get over the excitement of the wedding. Then an aircraft of the Queen's Flight (with Charles at the controls) took them to Gibraltar, where they boarded Britannia.

With 277 officers and men (plus the Band of the Royal Marines) to look after them, Charles and Diana spent two weeks sailing along the Italian coast and through the Greek

islands, stopping for a beach barbecue at Ithaca and to windsurf off Crete, where the Prince brought out his easel and painted. Idyllic is almost an inadequate word to describe the honeymoon which was to go on, with breaks, for three months.

And yet, right from the beginning, it was not as it seemed. Even as the champagne was being chilled for their first candlelit dinner, Diana realized, to her dismay, that they would not be alone. The ship's officers would be dining with them. It would be the same every night of the cruise and Charles, a naval officer, thoroughly enjoyed the company. When he wasn't playing deck hockey or flying a kite, the Prince was sitting on the veranda deck immersed 'with pure joy' in one of the Van der Post novels.

As he wrote to a friend: 'All I can say is that marriage is very jolly and it is extremely nice being together on Britannia. Diana dashes about chatting up all the sailors and the cooks in the galley, etc.'

(Above): *Lost in thought: A brief moment alone together for the newlyweds on Britannia. Diana came home with many happy memories and a few doubts.*
(Opposite): *A glowing Princess arriving in Gibraltar to begin her honeymoon on the Royal Yacht Britannia.*

But the Prince had already noticed that his bride was often ill at ease and displaying something he had never seen during their courtship: sudden changes in mood. It puzzled him. He seems to have been blind to Diana's need to be alone with him. Years later, when the marriage was effectively over, the memories of those honeymoon evenings on the yacht still made her unhappy.

From the Greek islands, they made for the Suez Canal where Egypt's President Anwar Sadat came on board for a formal dinner held in his honour. It was an official occasion tailor-made for a new and uncertain Princess of Wales: the President was a genial man and his wife Jihan was the daughter of a Sheffield history teacher. But it was Charles's new cuff links that caught Diana's attention. They bore a motif of the entwined initials 'CC'. As Diana suspected, they were a gift from Camilla Parker Bowles.

Another shock was to follow. When the newlyweds were sitting together organizing their schedules, two photographs of Camilla fell from between the pages of Charles's open diary. If these really were the final exchanges of an old love affair, one has to question the insensitivity of the Prince of Wales in letting his young bride see them, even though he insisted that they were merely tokens of a friendship that was over by then.

Over it may well have been, but to Diana, Mrs Parker Bowles was as good as with them on honeymoon. It was the trigger for the eating disorder that became a daily feature on Britannia.

Diana's description of her illness is harrowing: 'Appalling, absolutely appalling. It was rife, four times a day on the yacht. Anything I could find I would gobble up and then I would be sick two minutes later. I was very tired. So, of course, that slightly got the mood swings going in the sense that one minute I would be happy, the next I would be blubbing. I cried my eyes out on my honeymoon. I was so tired, for all the wrong reasons.'

Certainly, staff on board were puzzled by her appetite. She would visit the galley to eat bowls of ice cream and would ask for snacks between meals.

And yet the honeymoon was far from being all bad. In the occasional inconsistencies which pepper Diana's recollections, she found happiness at times, even in the company of Van der Post's writings, which Charles read to her, sitting on the highest hill on the Balmoral estate after their return to Scotland. 'I did my tapestry and he

was blissfully happy. As long as he was happy that was fine,' she said.

The key to this recollection of happiness is that Diana, for once, had the Prince to herself. Her dislocated childhood had created a woman who needed to be showered with affection. But already, Charles's friends were describing her as being 'obsessive' about Camilla. Tragically, the Prince's response to the edginess and moods that the thought of Camilla was causing was to go out of his way to sidestep the moments of intimacy for which Diana longed.

It was a tragedy compounded by Charles's inability to respond sensitively to something he had quite simply never encountered before. He believed her problems

(Opposite and above): *Charles and Diana arrive in Scotland to finish their honeymoon at Balmoral. For once, she had him all to herself.*

would pass. All she needed was time to adapt to her new role. And, publicly, she certainly was.

Charles and Diana's first official engagement together as a married couple was in Wales in October 1981, when the Prince presented his bride to the people. The result was some of the most amazing (and, for Charles, unexpected) scenes. It was the birth of a new phenomenon: Di-mania. There was a clamour of excitement throughout the visit and the massive crowds made it obvious whom they saw as the new star of the royal show.

All his life, the Prince had had to get used to public curiosity and crowds anxious to see him close up. But something different happened in Wales. They were hardly interested in him at all, but in his wife. Being virtually ignored had never happened to the Prince before. Just four months after the wedding, he found himself playing second fiddle to his bride.

Curiously, Diana did not even look her best. The Princess was pregnant, though the world would not know it until the following month. On top of the bouts of illness caused by her bulimia, she was suffering from morning sickness. Despite her pregnancy, Diana's weight had plum-

meted. She looked thin, but her girlish charm and uncertainty made the crowds warm to her. It was painfully obvious to Charles that his wife was the centre of attention.

If he was jealous, he didn't show it – yet. Diana acknowledged that he was concerned at the effect the vast crowds would have on her and he was doing his best to help her through the ordeal.

Just months before, she had been an unknown girl looking after children in a kindergarten. Now, pregnant with William and having lost a lot of weight through bulimia (which had not been diagnosed at that stage), she was the object of adulation on a scale unprecedented in Britain. The Prince was by no means sure that she could cope.

Yet despite her anxieties (at times the very thought of appearing in public made her tremble) Diana was showing a remarkable resilience as well as a special talent with people. In Cardiff, she put on one of those sparkling public performances that were to become her trademark. She made her first speech partly in Welsh at Cardiff City Hall. It went down well and she blushingly received the freedom of the city.

On walkabouts, the crowd on Charles's side of the street would groan, while shrieks of pleasure and outstretched hands would come from Diana's side. The Prince found himself apologizing for not having enough wives to go round. He tried to be light-hearted about it. 'I seem to do nothing but collect flowers [for Diana] these days. I know my role,' he said. At first, Diana didn't recognize the negative impact that her success, which would soon reach mega-star status, was having on Charles. But how could she? For the moment, the new Princess was merely the newest and brightest thing to happen to British public life for generations.

While Wales marked the beginning of Di-mania, the royal visit in spring 1983 to Australia and New Zealand, Diana's first foreign trip, generated even more excitement. One million people turned out to see her, despite murmurs of Republicanism.

The crowds were the biggest Charles had ever seen. He knew without any doubt that they all wanted to see Diana, not him. And by then he resented it. He was not alone. Other senior royals were also noting that they never got such receptions and were disturbed to find that the newcomer in their midst was outshining them all.

To understand their discomfort at Diana's success is not difficult, according to a senior royal aide: 'Each member of the Royal Family sees himself or herself as a superstar. They come together only for Trooping the Colour and Christmas, and that's the way they like it. They each like their own spotlight.' Charles, however, was being dazzled by the spotlight on Diana.

Other royal firsts were being notched up: when they went to Australia in 1983, it was as a family. As the plans for the four-week official tour were being finalized, the Australian Prime Minister Malcolm Fraser had written out of the blue to suggest that they brought 9-month-old Prince William. So they did, and extended the trip by two weeks to include New Zealand.

(Right): *The crowds braved the weather to see Diana during the married couple's first official trip together to Wales in October 1981.*

(Opposite): *This off-the-shoulder gown shows Diana's dramatic weight loss. On Britannia, she would go to the galley between meals to eat bowls of ice cream, and would then make herself sick, often up to four times a day.*

*A heavily pregnant Diana with Prince Charles at a polo match at Smith's Lawn, Windsor,
in June 1982. Just five days later, their son William was born.*

During the trip, it was easy to see the pleasure people were getting from Diana's mere presence. It was Diana, and Diana alone, who was generating forces of which she did not know herself capable.

Diana saw the impact on Charles of what was happening and worried about it. As she said: 'Everybody always said when we were in the car: "Oh, we're on the wrong side, we want to see her, we don't want to see him." That's all we could hear when we went through these crowds. He wasn't used to that and nor was I.

'He took it out on me. He was jealous. I understood the jealousy but I couldn't explain that I didn't ask for it (the adulation). I kept saying: "You've married someone and whoever you'd have married would have been of interest for the clothes, how she handles this, that and the other."'

Some might say that Diana's later recollection of jealousy is exaggerated. As she was to tell her beautician and friend Janet Filderman, the Prince had been 'very protective' on the tour. While Charles was undoubtedly resentful at being eclipsed by his wife, his overriding attitude was one of concern for her. She had, after all, made him supremely happy by giving him a healthy son and heir.

William had been born on the warm evening of 21 June 1982, with a fascinated Prince of Wales at Diana's bedside. And although a decade later when her life was at its bleakest she complained that the baby was induced to fit in with Charles's polo diary, the Princess had at first taken as a good omen the fact that William's birthday was a very special date: the longest day of the year.

Diana was right to believe that one way to keep her husband's mind on the marriage, and not on Camilla,

A student kisses Princess Diana's hand during a walkabout in Melbourne in March 1983. The six-week trip to Australia and New Zealand was another royal first: 9-month-old Prince William came, too, instead of the usual practice of leaving the children at home in the care of nannies.

(Above): *Charles looks on as Diana tends to William during his christening.*
(Opposite): *The Princess was being treated for depression but the official portrait of mother and child shows there were times when she was blissfully happy.*

was through children, for nothing was more important to him than the Succession.

William was born at 9.03pm, weighing 7lb 1½oz, and it was almost three hours later when Charles left the hospital and went home to Kensington Palace.

He was drained but also desperately relieved, because when Diana had been three months pregnant and obsessively preoccupied with Camilla, she had made the first of several apparent suicide attempts by throwing herself down the stairs at Sandringham.

The day after William's birth, Charles wrote to his friends Hugh and Emilie van Cutsem: 'I got back here just before midnight, utterly elated but quite shattered. I can't tell you how excited and proud I am. He really does look surprisingly appetizing and has sausage fingers just like mine.' But despite the broad public smiles, there were renewed private problems when Diana emerged from hospital carrying her new baby. She was treated for chronic depression, seeing several psychologists and psychiatrists.

Much later, she believed she had been suffering from both the effects of bulimia and post-natal depression. She never stopped believing that Camilla's shadow had a lot to do with her health problems. But at the time, she and her husband were confused by her unhappiness.

The royals were content to believe that it would pass. And, eventually, it did. By the time she was pregnant with Harry, Diana was, once again, very happy.

She was writing regularly to the Duchess of Kent, who had become a friend soon after the engagement, and the Duchess says that what struck her from Diana's words was 'how supremely happy she was in the beginning when the children were born'.

Like many women, the Princess was at her happiest when she was pregnant and was to regret having only two sons because, from the time she was a little girl, she wanted, fairy tale-style, 'lots of children'.

When she sent a framed picture of herself and her newborn son to Maudie Pendrey, the housekeeper at

Althorp, the Princess wrote: 'William has brought us such happiness and contentment and consequently I can't wait for masses more.'

In another letter, thanking Mrs Pendrey and her husband Ainsley, the butler, for a gift of knitted cardigans for William, she said: 'Hopefully, all of us will be able to come to Althorp before Christmas as I'd so like to show off my marvellous husband and son to you both!'

These blissful letters show that if Diana really was suffering from post-natal blues as well as depression caused by bulimia, there were times when she was free from both and very happy with her marriage.

Harry's birth on 15 September 1984, was somewhat different from William's, not only because Diana did not suffer a recurrence of the post-natal depression she had suffered with her first child but because the royal excitement was relatively muted.

Diana never forgot her husband's dismay. As she recalled: 'Charles always wanted a girl… Harry was a boy. His first comment was: "Oh God, it's a boy;" his second: "And he's even got red hair." '

The Prince tempered his disappointment by noting, as he told friends, that his new son was 'a fine little chap'. And in those early years, he was probably closer to the infant Harry than to his heir.

By the time of Prince Harry's christening both Diana and Charles were delighted with their young family, captured in this official portrait by Lord Snowdon.

Charles's friends cast doubt on Diana's assertion that his disappointment was deep. They suggest that she assumed this to be the case because of her father's bitter disappointment when she was born his third daughter and not the son and heir he craved.

The Prince had certainly hoped for a daughter and Diana had concealed from him the knowledge, learned from a scan well into the pregnancy, that her baby was a boy. Curiously for a young woman prone to attacks of depression, Diana coped remarkably well with her secret of the baby's sex. If anything should have depressed her, it was that. And yet it didn't.

The reason was that she knew her husband would quickly come to terms with it and, crucially, she believed that his desire for a daughter would strengthen the marriage and diminish Camilla's relevance. But a daughter never came.

This delightful sequence of pictures gives a real sense of the Waleses' relaxed family life. Photographer Tim Graham was finding it difficult to hold the attention of the two young Princes during a photo shoot at Highgrove – until Charles stepped in. He played peek-a-boo with his handkerchief and pulled funny faces to captivate the boys for long enough to get this very special portrait.

Chapter 7

HER BELOVED BOYS

Soon after William was born, Diana insisted that Prince Charles spend one hour each morning in the nursery with their son. Charles could not understand Diana's need for him to have this constant contact with the baby. But the 21-year-old Princess would not be put off. She knew what kind of family life she wanted and, in this particular battle of family versus duty, she won.

It was agreed that Charles would spend from 9am to 10am in the nursery.

He began enthusiastically enough but, of course, it didn't last. Before long, the hour had been reduced to forty-five minutes. Then the pressures on his time reduced it to half an hour and, as one intimate source says: 'Eventually, you were lucky to find him there after 9.15am.'

The old retainers and courtiers knew what the problem was. The Prince had been brought up by nannies and had never had the normal, rough and tumble childhood that his wife was determined to give their children.

There were nannies in the Princess's upbringing, too, of course, but in her home in Norfolk there had always been a real family atmosphere, even after her mother had left when Diana was six.

The pivotal difference was that for the Spencer children, especially Diana, it was natural to look after each other. It is clear to those who have been close to the Prince all his life that he has never really bonded with his siblings, let alone his parents.

It was this family bonding that Diana was trying to establish, not only between Charles and his sons but between the boys themselves.

In 1996, she took William and Harry to the North London studio of photographer John Swannell to sit for

(Opposite): *Playing with 8-month-old William. Princess Diana considered family bonding to be as important as royal tradition.*
(Above): *Diana's hands-on approach to child rearing, with shy toddler Harry (a month short of his second birthday) in Majorca during a holiday with the Spanish royal family in August 1986. She was determined to make her sons part of her life, rather than being 'hidden upstairs with the governess'.*

this Christmas card photograph. The shoot took twice as long as planned because the boys kept messing up their mother's carefully combed hair. 'I thought at the time: "What a wonderful relationship she has with them,"' says Swannell.

Diana saw it as central that family came before protocol. But Charles, as one close observer says, 'simply couldn't understand what she was doing'. The Princess was dismayed but not deterred by her husband's reluctance. It fired her with an unshakable determination to make sure that her children did not suffer from the same family remoteness and resulting unhappy childhood as their father.

Charles was the living example of what she was trying to avoid for William and Harry. She knew his relationship with his parents had never been easy. It is ironic that, though her parents had divorced, Diana felt totally loved by them both, yet while the Queen and the Duke of Edinburgh have had a rock-steady marriage Charles grew up feeling unloved and misunderstood by each of them.

The Princess hated the way her husband feared Prince Philip, who seemed to rule the Royals while the Queen took a passive path through the family's ups and downs. Philip had been responsible for sending Charles to Gordonstoun, a school he hated.

Diana didn't want her boys to suffer the same traumas. She put the mistakes in Charles's upbringing, as she saw it, down to duty taking precedence over family life. She understood it because her father had been an equerry to two monarchs and she was raised next door to the Royals at Sandringham.

However, even the Princess had to admit that, excluding the problems of his dwindling morning visits to the nursery, Charles did make a big effort to shed the stiff traditions of his royal upbringing. But she did things with the boys which her husband would never have considered. In retrospect, even he recognizes that, in this respect, the monarchy owes her a huge debt in its fight for public approval.

Who but Diana would have taken both boys to meet young homeless people at a Centrepoint hostel in 1995 and to visit the down-and-outs at The Passage, a church-run

This photograph took twice as long to shoot, as the boys kept messing up their mother's carefully combed hair.

5-year-old Harry's first day at Wetherby School, West London, in September 1989, where he joined William, aged seven. Charles had wanted his sons to be educated at home by governesses, as he had been. But Diana was determined that the boys would go to school with other children, as she had. Yet again, she won.

refuge in Westminster? Who but Diana would have taken 9-year-old William, the heir-in-line to the throne, to visit her friend Adrian Ward-Jackson dying of Aids in hospital?

Who but Diana would have included the 12-year-old Harry on her regular visits to London's Royal Brompton Hospital to chat to cystic fibrosis patients? The young Prince brought along a computer game and played it with the patients, sitting on their beds. He was an old hand – three years before, he had played cards with the homeless at The Passage.

Charles was at first uncertain about introducing his sons at such a young age to the more unpleasant aspects of life, but he sensibly came to accept it and later even approve of it. He saw how it was rounding out and shaping them, and everyone around him could see how much the public applauded this new approach to royal upbringing.

The Prince had wanted the early years of William and Harry to be in the strict, though kind, hands of Mabel Anderson, his Scottish nanny. Charles had been in her charge in the nursery while being taught by governesses at Buckingham Palace until he was almost eight, when he went to Hill House school in Knightsbridge. He wanted his children to be similarly educated at home in their early years.

But Diana wanted them to go to school with other children, just as she had. Yet again, as with his nursery visits and with their names (Prince Charles wanted William to be called Arthur and Harry to be called Albert, which became their second names), the Princess won.

To the young Princess, still on a steep and dizzying learning curve about life within the Royal Family, it was vital for the boys to grow up to be comfortable with all kinds of people. She viewed with horror the possibility of them being 'hidden upstairs with the governess'. Charles seldom saw his mother when he was a boy.

Diana's approach was to 'hug my children to death. I get into bed with them at night and say "Who loves you most in the whole world?" and they always say "Mummy". I feed them love and affection – it's so important'.

At the same time, Diana was careful never to lose sight of the other main objective in her life: bringing up William and Harry to respect, understand and continue the 1,000-year tradition of the monarchy.

Diana and 9-year-old William at Wimbledon in 1991.

She would say: 'It's very important to me that my sons have a good relationship with the Queen.' Carolan Brown, the Princess's fitness trainer for five years until 1994, remembers Diana telling her: 'The boys are going to see Granny today. I'm so glad they like her.' Some people may still contend that Diana destabilized the monarchy, but she was acutely conscious of its vital role in the life of the country. She did her utmost, in her own way, to promote it.

Diana was determined that her boys would grow up to be comfortable with both paupers and princes, but they would never be allowed to forget how important it was that they 'understood and respected the tradition of which they were part'.

At the same time, she did not shrink from being firm. Jenni Rivett, the Princess's fitness trainer for seven years, remembers how William annoyed his mother one morning when she was working out at the Chelsea Harbour Club gym. Diana thundered at him: 'Just go away, William, you're being irritating.' He did.

The young Princes played an important and, in retrospect, touchingly poignant role in Diana's loyal defence of the Prince of Wales when her sycophants poked fun at him, wrongly imagining she would approve.

'The Princess never liked that sort of thing and would rebuke them saying: "Remember that he's the father of my children,"' says Roberto Devorik, the Argentine fashion entrepreneur who was her close friend for fifteen years.

Diana enjoyed lunchtime meetings with Devorik's friends, including the French film star Isabelle Huppert, whom she met when the actress was in London playing Mary, Queen of Scots. Diana told her: 'Who knows, one day you might end up playing Diana, Princess of Wales.'

But these glamorous gatherings never took precedence over her sons. Once, she was due to join Madonna at Devorik's apartment, but Diana cancelled, he recalls, 'because it would have meant being unable to take the boys back to school'.

The Princess's close friend Susie Kassem, wife of financier Tariq Kassem, says the boys were 'permanently' important to her. They came first. Often they were there when Susie lunched at Kensington Palace and they were always 'utterly charming'. She found William 'drop dead gorgeous' and Harry was 'really good news, too'. Susie's son Kristian nicknamed Diana 'the yummy mummy'.

It was the baseball-caps-and-McDonald's informality of William and Harry's upbringing that was so different from anything that had gone before in the Royal Family. The famous visits to Thorpe Park and Alton Towers, shrieking on those white-knuckle rides, were only a part of the way Diana steered them to know the real world.

Once when she visited William at boarding school, the Princess jumped exuberantly from bed to bed along the row in the dormitory as all the other pupils looked on in amazement. This was all part of Diana's training of her boys for the world outside the palace. She wanted them to understand the reason for their privileged position and why some people suffer and struggle, but she also wanted them to have fun and behave like normal boys, despite the responsibility of their roles.

The Princess loved motherhood perhaps more than anything. Like her bulimia, that, too, had its roots in her childhood. She was always telling friends how much she wanted more children, particularly a daughter. 'She often used to comment on how beautiful Fergie's two daughters were,' remembers Jenni Rivett.

When Diana held a recital at Kensington Palace late in 1992, the 10-year-old William watched through the door as thirty people arrived for dinner and then filed into one of the sitting rooms for the concert. Among the guests was Harold King, founder-director of the City Ballet of London, of which the Princess was patron from 1983 until 1996. Diana grinned at her son as she told King: 'William wants to watch this but I've told him if he falls asleep he's going to get a smack.'

King says: 'We all sat down, it was terribly quiet and then the baritone started. It was only a small room so his voice just boomed across it, really loud. William had to sit there impeccably behaved while his mother, in fits of laughter, tried to cover her hand with her mouth. But it was no use.'

You can easily understand why Diana became so inflamed when, after she and Charles parted in 1992, he introduced his personal assistant Tiggy Legge-Bourke as a part-time surrogate mother. Once again, it looked to the Princess as though a love which was vital to her life was being diluted, even stolen. She raged that Tiggy always seemed to be having fun with the boys.

Diana reasoned that if she didn't need a man to help her look after the boys when they were with her (custody,

Diana and 9-year-old Harry get soaked in 1993 at Thorpe Park.
The Princess loved these informal days out.

*Laughing and joking with William, eight, and Harry, almost six, over lunch
at the Cirque du Soleil, South Bank, London, in August 1990.*

including holidays, was shared), why did Charles need a woman to help him?

But despite this, Diana's way was working. No moment illustrates her success more movingly than the day she locked herself in a bathroom during a particular marital crisis. William heard her crying and pushed tissues under the door.

Charles, meanwhile, was teaching his sons the ways of the countryside. He taught them to shoot, fish and hunt, and encouraged them to share his love of painting, music and the theatre. The Prince often attends performances by the Royal Shakespeare Company at Stratford-on-Avon, and William and Harry have also been spotted with him.

The difficulties in the marriage, especially after the separation in December 1992, served to change Charles into a rather different father from the one who was reluctant to spend time in the nursery all those years ago.

The children's holiday time was injected with a definite element of competition. Diana took them to the Caribbean, the Rocky Mountains and, on that final holiday last summer, to St Tropez. Charles has taken them skiing in Klosters, cruising in the Mediterranean and on safari in Africa, but he also likes them to enjoy traditional pursuits in the tranquillity of Balmoral.

As a separated parent, Charles has found himself working at a new informality with his sons, which they enjoy. There is frequent horseplay and, when they were younger, he would read to them in bed, especially Rudyard Kipling's *Just So* stories.

None of this has come as easily to the Prince as it does to other fathers because of what has been described as a 'gulf of misunderstanding' caused by the pressures of public life. Expressing affection is difficult for the Royal Family, including Charles. But, thanks to Diana, it comes easily to the two young Princes.

Take the skiing holiday in Switzerland in the winter of 1997. On the final evening, Charles gave a dinner party in the Walserhof Hotel at Klosters. Suddenly, there was the earnest figure of Harry on his feet making a thank-you speech to his father for giving them a terrific holiday. As he finished, he rushed to Charles and smothered him in hugs and kisses until, in mock embarrassment, the Prince begged for mercy.

How different things might have been if Charles could have done that to his father. Above all, this was a moment that showed the Prince of Wales the value of Diana's hugging philosophy.

It was the best possible demonstration that, by the time of her death, the Princess had been responsible for putting in place a welcome new style of upbringing for the future King and his brother – and one on which there is no going back.

After their separation in 1992, Diana and Charles vied with each other to give the boys memorable holidays. (Top): The Prince enjoys traditional royal holidays at Balmoral, pictured in spring 1994 with 9-year-old Harry and 11-year-old William. (Above): During their final trip in the summer of 1997, the Princess shared a jet ski with 12-year-old Harry off St Tropez.

Chapter 8

THE ROAD TO REDEMPTION

henever it came, the nightmare was the same in every detail. Diana watches as the crown is placed on Charles's head. He adjusts it. Then the unidentified figures officiating at the Coronation move across to her with another crown and lower it onto her head. But despite repeated efforts, it will not stay on. Instead, it slips down over her face and starts to suffocate her.

Only one or two of the Princess of Wales's closest friends knew of the Coronation nightmare and how it plagued her night after night in the years after the death of her father, Earl Spencer, in 1992.

The man to whom the Princess took her nightmare was Dr Alan McGlashan, a dream counsellor and Jungian psychoanalyst who went to his grave in May 1997, taking the professional secrets of Diana's disturbed sleep with him.

Whatever McGlashan told the Princess about her nightmare failed to satisfy her and even confused her. She stopped going to him, probably because of his over-riding philosophy that dreams try to tell us about the dark side of ourselves which, consciously, we prefer not to acknowledge.

Diana believed that if there was a dark message in her Coronation dream it was about her own sense of inadequacy and failure. For she first had the dream when she knew she had lost her contest with Camilla Parker Bowles for Charles's love and undivided attention.

She dreamed it most often not when she was at her weakest with bulimia and crying for help with her half-hearted suicide attempts, but in the years after her separation from Charles in December 1992 when she had begun the process of hauling herself out of the pit of despair. She dreamed it not when her life was at its bleakest but when she found herself growing stronger both mentally and physically. Eventually, she began to see the Coronation dream as an expression of regret for what might have been, especially in regard to Camilla. For every time the rejuvenated, stronger Diana woke

(Opposite): *At a banquet in Auckland, New Zealand, in April 1983. Diana was by now in the grip of bulimia and had already made three half-hearted suicide bids.* (Above): *The tension between Charles and Diana became obvious in public during their 1988 tour of Australia.*

from the dream, she knew that she could have beaten off the other woman and retained Charles's love if only she had not been so young and inexperienced.

She looked back with more than regret at what she regarded as the behaviour of a demented young woman who had taken a penknife from Charles's desk and used it to cut her chest and arms, who had slashed her hand by deliberately plunging it through a glass case, and who had thrown herself down the stairs when she was pregnant with William.

The resurrected Diana felt angry that her own naïvety meant she had failed to fight fire with fire. While Camilla was whatever the Prince wanted her to be at any time – sometimes mistress, sometimes wit, sometimes counsellor – Diana realized that she had gone about trying to hold on to Charles in exactly the wrong way.

The big question, of course, is could she have changed anything, bearing in mind her bulimia and depression? The medical answer is probably not.

On the other hand, Diana, recalling that first chill in her stomach when she suspected there was another woman in Charles's life, told her friend Roberto Devorik that had she been, say, twenty-five instead of nineteen when she became engaged, she would have been wise enough to see off Camilla. She reflected that 'keeping herself tidy' (the aristocratic expression for staying a virgin), with almost no experience of men until Charles, had put her at a devastating disadvantage.

Diana was angry with herself for allowing her despair to degenerate into an eating disorder, which only made things worse. Far from capturing the Prince of Wales's attention, he displayed a total inability to cope with her depression and distress. His response to her outbursts was, wherever possible, to absent himself. And the person whose comfort he most often sought when he fled from the sobbing, sometimes shrieking, Diana was Camilla, the very woman the Princess believed to be at the root of all her troubles.

To understand the origins of that recurring nightmare it is necessary to go back to one of the last days of the Royal couple's extended honeymoon. Three months after their

Once she had been so proud of her figure. Now, whenever possible she would hide it, as shown in this picture taken on a visit to Cirencester in 1986 to watch Prince Charles play polo.

wedding day in July 1981, the Prince's personal secretary and old Navy chum Michael Colborne took a phone call from Balmoral, where Charles and Diana were staying.

That evening, the fatherly, softly spoken Colborne boarded the sleeper train at King's Cross station, London. It was breakfast time when he arrived at the castle. His brief from the Prince was straightforward. Diana was upset and had been crying. He was to sit with her, and talk if she wanted to, while Charles went out shooting.

All day until teatime, when Diana went for a walk, Colborne sat with the Princess. Some of the time she sobbed or buried her head in her hands. Sandwiches were sent in for lunch.

The cause of the upset was, as ever, Camilla, the woman she later referred to as either 'the Rottweiler' or 'the Presence'. The Princess's weight was plummeting so fast that she had that very day handed her loose wedding ring to Charles, who passed it on to Colborne with instructions to have it made smaller.

The young Princess's predicament can be vividly seen in her husband's decision to send for his personal secretary, albeit a popular and trusted figure, to 'babysit' his upset wife so he could go out for the day. If Diana was naïve about handling her husband in those early days, what does this say of the Prince's handling of her?

On the royal train back to London, Charles was also, inevitably after what had happened, feeling rather low. Some of his staff and friends who had been at Balmoral gathered in his carriage and he initiated a discussion on… relationships.

Soon the Princess would begin the long process of analysis by food disorder specialists, including Guy's Hospital psychiatrist Dr Maurice Lipsedge (who some years earlier had treated her older sister Sarah for anorexia) and the dream counsellor Dr McGlashan. The Prince's guru, Sir Laurens Van der Post, had also been whisked up to Balmoral to see her, with little effect.

During the autumn of that first year of marriage, various psychologists and doctors visited Diana at Buckingham Palace. Though they recommended tranquillizers, she resisted taking them because she was pregnant and also because she realized that what she needed could not be prescribed by doctors. Through the debilitating fog of her eating disorder and melancholy, she knew she needed something much more intimate and secure.

The affair with Charles had in reality resumed by 1984 when Camilla, Tom, nine, and Laura, five, accompanied Andrew to Buckingham Palace to receive his OBE.

By the time the Princess threw herself down the stairs at Sandringham, when she was three months pregnant with William, she was, as she said: 'Just so desperate. I knew what was wrong with me but nobody else around me understood. I needed rest and to be looked after inside my house and for people to understand the torment and anguish going on in my head. It was a desperate cry for help.'

Her royal life was not so much the goldfish bowl once famously described by her father-in-law Prince Philip but imprisonment behind toughened glass. She could see what was happening to her but was unable to do anything about it. Nor did anyone in the palace seem to understand when she tried to tell them about her domestic problems. Privately, especially through the early years of the marriage, Diana believed that the Queen was sympathetic but was loyally accepting her son's word that the marriage was breaking down not because of another woman but

because of the Princess's eating disorder and consequent erratic behaviour. 'I don't know what my husband fed the Queen,' Diana said. 'He definitely told her about my bulimia and she told everybody that was the reason why our marriage had cracked up ["because of Diana's eating")]and that it must be so difficult for Charles.'

Diana didn't *blame* Camilla for loving Charles – she understood that well enough because she loved him herself. She blamed Camilla for destabilizing her marriage. Years later, this would be intensified to 'the destruction of my family'.

Charles insisted then, just as he later did in his interview on television with Jonathan Dimbleby in June 1994, that Camilla was out of his life from the moment of his wedding until 1986 when the marriage had 'irretrievably broken down'. But throughout these crucial early years, Diana could not bring herself to believe him.

As Diana recalled: 'I once heard him on the phone in his bath saying: "Whatever happens, I will always love you." I told him later that I had listened at the door and we had a filthy row.'

The entire romantic arrangement, it must be said, was bizarre by any standards of normal family life. The Parker

Bowleses were ostensibly happily married. The debonair Colonel (later Brigadier) Andrew Parker Bowles was a friend of Charles and one-time boyfriend of Princess Anne. And there was Camilla bringing up her two small children, Tom (one of Charles's godsons) and Laura.

In most circles, for a man to tell his bride that his romance with the woman who had become the wife of an old friend was over would be treated with incredulity that it had ever even started. More so for him to reveal that later he had resumed cuckolding his friend when his own marriage was seemingly beyond repair. Yet there was only one raised eyebrow in royal circles: Diana's.

The Princess could hardly believe it when, in one furious argument, her husband tersely asked: 'Do you seriously expect me to be the first Prince of Wales in history not to have a mistress?'

It was the obsequious lack of censure or even disapproval of Charles's adultery in royal circles that burned into Diana. It seemed to her that no one cared; that everyone thought she was overreacting. Poor Diana was 'ill'. It felt like a conspiracy.

When she asked for help from courtiers and the Royal Family, she said that they always told her she was imagining

things and that the relationship with Camilla was in the past. She could not accept that. The tragedy of those early, difficult years was that Diana knew what was going wrong but didn't know how to put it right. She knew that Charles had fallen in love with her because she was funny, loving and sympathetic but, within weeks of their marriage, she was suffering severe mood swings caused by bulimia.

She could see the effect it was having on her husband. She confided in her friend, the beautician Janet Filderman: 'My temper tantrums are driving him away. He doesn't understand that I need a good cry.'

When, as an effect of the bulimia, she fainted while walking around the Expo '86 exhibition in Vancouver with the Prince, his reaction was to tick her off. 'He said I could have passed out quietly somewhere else, behind a door,' she recalled.

And what was the Princess to make of the scene that greeted her in 1990 when she took a helicopter of the Queen's Flight to Highgrove, their country home, to pay her husband an impromptu visit after he had broken his arm playing polo?

The surprise was not as she intended, for there was Camilla plumping up his pillows. It was one of the inci-

Their marriage at breaking point, Charles and Diana look strained during a tour of Cameroon in March 1990.

dents that made her say of her husband's long-time mistress: 'I see in her what I would not want to see in my best friend or in myself.'

Camilla predated Diana in Charles's life, of course, by almost a decade. The story of the former Camilla Shand's first meeting with the Prince of Wales in 1972 is well-known. She introduced herself by telling him that her great-grandmother, Alice Keppel, had been the mistress of his great-great-grandfather Edward VII and ended with '… so how about it, Sir?'

Charles saw a lot of Camilla for some months before he sailed to the Caribbean as an officer aboard HMS Minerva. Seven months later, he received a letter from her with the news that she was to marry his good friend, Andrew Parker Bowles – conveniently as it turned out.

Five years and two children into the Parker Bowles marriage, Camilla resumed her affair with Prince Charles. Diana always believed that it was never interrupted again.

Chapter 9

THE END OF THE FAIRYTALE

No one could deny it was the climax of one of the most glittering black tie parties of the year. Pop singer Phil Collins led the 600 guests invited to Buckingham Palace by the Queen in a rousing chorus of Happy Birthday in honour of the 40-year-old Prince of Wales.

And yet of all the memories carried away by party-goer Kay King as the celebration broke up just before 3am in November 1988, the one that stuck with her was how Diana and Charles's separate sets of friends were 'so very distant with each other, hardly talking all evening'.

It was as Kay Seth-Smith that Mrs King, now forty-five, had employed Lady Diana Spencer as a nursery assistant at the Young England Kindergarten in Pimlico a decade earlier. She and her businessman husband were among a number of old friends whom Diana had invited to Charles's birthday celebration. Even on such a night of champagne, glamour and dancing to the Dark Blues band who had played at the Prince's 21st birthday, the Kings

could feel the uneasy marital rift that was being hinted at in royal circles, and could see how people were taking sides.

It would not be many more birthdays before the animosity would break out into open warfare and descend into one of the most unsavoury episodes in royal history, with exposures of intimate telephone conversations and allegations of bugging and dirty tricks that would not have seemed out of place in Richard Nixon's Washington. As with all wars, the big question is: Who started it? (We will come later to who won it...)

Undoubtedly, Diana began the open hostilities by exposing, in devastating detail, the wretchedness of her marriage and the coldness of the Royal Family, as she saw it when feeling at rock bottom, in Andrew Morton's book, *Diana, Her True Story*, which was published in June 1992.

The jagged-edged conflict that followed was mutually embarrassing, debilitating and humiliating, not to mention

(Above): The tension shows as Diana leaves a Merseyside hospice in June 1992. It was her first
public engagement after the publication of Andrew Morton's controversial biography of the Princess.
(Opposite): The Prince and Princess of Wales on an official trip to Australia in 1985.

potentially destructive to the monarchy. But Diana never believed she had really fired the first shot. 'They did,' she said. 'They' were Charles's circle, and Diana felt entirely justified in going public because she insisted that the initial act of hostility had come from them.

Ironically, this also involved a birthday party – one which never took place. The Prince had suggested throwing a party at Highgrove for Diana's 30th birthday in July 1991. She declined and he felt insulted.

Within a few days, details of the snub were leaked to the media as a way of demonstrating what a difficult life Charles had with a petulant and miserable Princess who had refused a birthday party from her loving husband.

Diana saw it somewhat differently. She had long felt abandoned by Charles who had, by 1986, renewed his affair with Camilla Parker Bowles. The Princess had discovered a kind of love in the arms of James Hewitt, the handsome Life Guards officer who had helped her overcome her fear of horses.

Over lunch with her old friend Roberto Devorik at Geale's, a smart fish-and-chip restaurant in West London's Notting Hill, Diana pointedly asked what he thought she represented to the public. He told her she was the epitome of fantasy, love and beauty.

'Wrong,' she declared. 'I'm the epitome of hypocrisy.' She was alluding to the public perception of her fairytale marriage compared with the sham it really was. In her eyes, for Charles to throw a birthday party for her would be more hypocritical than ever.

What most infuriated the Prince about the involvement of Diana and her friends in the Morton book was not its exposure of the emotional sterility of the monarchy, or even his shortcomings as a husband, but the outing of Camilla as his mistress. He was worried on Mrs Parker Bowles's account, not his own.

Diana knew well enough that she would come under fire for the Morton book, but she was prepared for it.

Her move had been a pre-emptive strike because her greatest fear was the possibility that, as her mother had discovered more than twenty years earlier, she could find herself fighting for custody of her children.

No one had mentioned divorce back then in 1992 but it was clear that Diana and Charles were heading for a separation. Throughout the Eighties, there had been rumours and gossip about Diana's mental state. She knew she was being written off not only as unstable, but unsuitable as a wife and, potentially, as a mother, too.

Her own mother Frances, who had left Diana's father Earl Spencer for the businessman Peter Shand Kydd, had lost custody of their children – Diana, her brother Charles and their two older sisters Sarah and Jane – in a bitter High Court battle in 1969, which led to the unfair allegation that she had abandoned her children.

The Princess was determined that this was never going to happen to her. Truth, she told herself, would not be the first casualty in this particular war.

To begin with there was no public response from Charles's side. But, nevertheless, a series of mysterious leaks soon began to seed the notion that Diana was betraying the monarchy.

The Princess took all the knocks with surprising dignity and even calm. 'I remember her growing up enormously in this period,' says the author and astrologer Felix Lyle, whom Diana consulted.

'It gave her a sense of power. She didn't just take a stand against the hypocrisy; she showed she could fight dirty, too.'

The then Archbishop of Canterbury, Robert Runcie, glimpsed a flash of Diana's growing resilience when they met at a state banquet. 'How goes it?' he asked. She replied: 'Well, I'm still as thick as a plank up here (tapping her forehead) but I've really got it down here (tapping her stomach).' She was saying she had the guts for a fight.

Within weeks of the publication of the Morton book, a transcript of the so-called 'Squidgy' tape recording of the Princess in intimate conversation with her friend James Gilbey arrived mysteriously in the Florida office of the American gossip rag, the *National Enquirer*. As expected, it was published and the story was circulated around the world.

A year earlier, several British newspapers had received an equally mysterious special delivery of the same typed transcript of the conversation, which had taken place around New Year 1989 when the Princess was at Sandringham with the Royal Family.

(Above): *A day out in Windsor Great Park for Charles, 9-year-old William and 7-year-old Harry at Easter 1992. By now, the boys were often seeing their parents separately.*

(Below): *Diana says her goodbyes on the doorstep to her friends Carolyn and William Bartholomew in June 1992. The public kiss was interpreted as the Princess's tacit approval of the involvement in the Morton book of Carolyn, her former flatmate.*

*The Waleses' poignant last joint Christmas card for 1992. This sombre
portrait of William and Harry by Lord Snowdon was a stark contrast
to the happy-go-lucky family shots of previous years.*

No one in Britain published it then. The sender was never known.

Three months after the Squidgy sensation, it was the turn of 'Camillagate', a tape of Prince Charles and Mrs Parker Bowles in an even more sensitive and intimate phone conversation. Both Charles and Diana had known of the tapes, but neither dreamed that they would ever be published. So who monitored the phone conversations and who sent the tapes to the Press?

No one took very seriously the claims of two radio hams, one saying that the Squidgy tape was the result of his tuning in by chance to the Princess's conversation and the other claiming the same about the Prince's late-night chat.

The scandal of the tapes was followed, almost inevitably, by the couple's separation. On the day of the split in December 1992, the dancer Wayne Sleep, a close friend of Diana's for years, phoned her to offer his sympathy.

She said: 'Don't worry, Wayne, I'm strong. I'm going to fight this.'

He says that she 'didn't sound like the gentle, soft, vulnerable person that I knew'.

While Diana confirmed the authenticity of Morton's account by allowing herself to be photographed publicly kissing one of his main sources, her former flatmate Carolyn Bartholomew, Charles's camp initially made no overt response. It later became known that Charles had ordered his friends to say nothing about his marriage, not even to defend him against accusations of being an uncaring husband.

Yet within a few months the Prince had entered into an arrangement with broadcaster Jonathan Dimbleby to write his life story and make a television documentary. Diana did not co-operate with this book, though she was invited to do so by Dimbleby when he met her for lunch at the home of a mutual friend, Baroness Jay. She believed that whatever she might tell Dimbleby, the resulting work was bound to be sympathetic to her husband. And it was.

Diana and her friends saw the picture portrayed in the book – of the Prince of Wales trapped in a marriage with a wife who was both unreasonable and unstable – as a revenge attack.

They were particularly incensed by the slant which had been put on a casual, innocent remark that the

Finally, came the one thing Diana had never wanted: divorce.
On 28 August 1996, the decree nisi was made absolute.

Certificate of making Decree Nisi Absolute (Divorce)

No 5029 of 1996

IN THE HIGH COURT OF JUSTICE
PRINCIPAL REGISTRY OF THE FAMILY DIVISION

Matrimonial cause proceeding in Principal Registry treated by virtue of section 42 of the Matrimonial and Family Proceedings Act 1984 as pending in a divorce county court

Between   HIS ROYAL HIGHNESS PRINCE CHARLES PHILIP

ARTHUR GEORGE THE PRINCE OF WALES

and   HER ROYAL HIGHNESS THE PRINCESS OF WALES

and

Petitioner
Respondent
Co-Respondent

Referring to the decree made in this cause

on the   15th   day of   July   1996.

whereby it was decreed that the marriage solemnised

on the   29th   day of   July   1981.

at the Cathedral Church of St Paul in the City and Diocese of London

between the petitioner and the respondent be dissolved unless sufficient cause be shown to the court within six weeks from the making thereof why the said decree

Diana and the Royals: (above) *she admired Princess Margaret as a role model;*
(below) *an exasperated Prince Philip tried to help;*
(opposite) *she always felt closest to Prince Andrew.*

teenage Diana, who was being courted by the Prince, had made to one of Charles's friends, Lord Romsey's wife, Penny.

Fourteen years later, certain members of Charles's circle had used Diana's simple words 'If I am lucky enough to be the Princess of Wales...' to plant in Dimbleby's mind the image of a girl behaving, as he wrote, 'as if she were auditioning for a central role in a costume drama'.

The implication was clear and linked up perfectly with the rumour mill that was suggesting that Diana had set her cap on that title from an early age and had remained a virgin to capture the most eligible bachelor in the land.

In the Eighties, her response to the pressures and unhappiness had been to succumb to bulimia in a drawn-out cry for help. It was then, the Princess believed, that she had first detected a lack of sympathy and even hostility from some of Charles's closest friends, including Hugh and Emilie van Cutsem and significantly, as it would later prove, the former Tory minister Nicholas Soames.

But by the early Nineties Diana had become a difficult and clever foe. When Charles went on television with Dimbleby to admit his adultery, a revelation that had been well trailed, Diana took care to look her sexiest in a wisp of a black dress at an engagement at the Serpentine Gallery that evening. It was one of many

talk. It was a major blow to the Princess when, in 1993, Lucia's husband was posted to Washington.

But the nature of the War of the Waleses had changed. It was no longer a tit-for-tat conflict based on a whispering campaign. Diana became convinced that she was the victim of a conspiracy to marginalize her in public life. She believed that she was being spied on and called in a company to sweep her apartment and telephone lines for bugs. Nothing was found.

What is not in doubt is that, as the perceived victim of the royal marriage, the Princess's popularity was seen as a threat to the Prince. The Palace was becoming anxious for him as supporters of the two protagonists flailed at each other. But by then, both sides were making costly mistakes. Charles's Dimbleby 1994 biography, with its incessant tone of blaming others for his problems had rebounded on him because it portrayed him as whingeing and weak.

Diana's *Panorama* interview the following year – which Charles's side saw as a counter-strike and in which she remarked memorably that 'there were three of us in this marriage' – was also a grave miscalculation.

Although it produced a wave of public sympathy (especially when the then Tory minister Nicholas Soames, one of Charles's best friends, described the Princess as being in the 'advanced stages of paranoia'), it speeded up the process towards the very thing Diana did not want: a divorce. Throughout the hostilities she, like Charles, was anxious not to be seen as the instigator of divorce proceedings. But Diana also felt that if it had to happen, it should wait until William and Harry were older.

Now, out of the blue, came an armistice. The shooting stopped overnight. It had to, for the sake of the children and for the sake of the monarchy. The heir to the throne and the mother of the future King had been in danger of destroying each other. They had also fought themselves to a standstill.

The final act of war was Buckingham Palace's decision, announced on 11 July 1996, cruelly to strip the Princess of her title, Her Royal Highness, as a penalty of the divorce.

So who won the War of the Waleses? The answer is neither of them. Charles knew he could never beat Diana in the publicity stakes and she knew she could never 'conquer the Establishment'. Emotionally, they were spent.

occasions when she was accused of deliberately upstaging the heir to the throne.

However, Diana was taking some hard knocks. In 1993, she began to find that planned visits abroad were being blocked unexpectedly. She wanted to visit British troops and refugees in Bosnia for the Red Cross (she was patron of Red Cross Youth), but was told that the Prince was planning a trip and that he took priority.

That September, she learned that she could not make a private visit to Dublin to meet the then Irish President Mary Robinson, a woman she admired. It was cancelled 'for security reasons', yet a few months later Charles went on an official visit to the Irish capital. A proposed trip by the Princess to a children's hospital in Moscow was similarly blocked.

Throughout these skirmishes, Diana found a mother figure in Lucia Flecha de Lima, the wife of the Brazilian ambassador in London, who made her Mayfair home a bolthole for the Princess.

She even kept a bed for her so that when Diana arrived in tears, they could lie down side by side and

In the months leading up to the divorce, an extraordinary change came over their relationship. Their lawyers may have been locked in combat, but the Waleses were not.

Diana suggested to the Prince that they work out their shared time with William and Harry personally and not through their offices as they had been doing. He happily agreed.

Early in 1997, six months after the divorce, the Prince suddenly arrived unannounced at Diana's apartment in Kensington Palace. He'd popped in, he explained, to use the loo. Diana's pleasure was almost childlike. She was thrilled that this could happen after all that they had been through.

Bubbling with excitement, she telephoned Simone Simmons, a friend who had become close in the years after Diana's separation from Charles in December 1992. She gasped: 'You'll never guess who just came to see me: my ex!'

The War of the Waleses was observed by the Royals with considerable anxiety and they were certainly relieved when it was over. Most of them had tried to stay well out of it, though there was considerable animosity towards Diana.

They accepted that, as the mother of a future King, she would never have set out to damage the monarchy, but they did not believe her assertion that she had never tried to 'rattle their cage'.

The word 'cage' was no accident. It was how the Princess of Wales saw the family's gilded life, especially her own, in the royal palaces. But she did not regard them all as enemies.

In particular, she both adored and admired Princess Margaret, even though Margo, as she called her Kensington Palace neighbour, would have been the last person to align herself with anyone taking issue with the monarchy.

For Diana, Margaret was a friend because she always knew where she stood with the Queen's sister, who had been 'wonderful to me from day one'. She also admired Margaret's civilized relationship with her former husband, Lord Snowdon. Margaret had managed to put her unsuccessful marriage behind her and, as a single mother, had reared two children who were now doing exactly what Diana eventually wanted for William and Harry: standing on their own feet as successes in their own right, not because of the mere accident of royal birth.

Margaret would never have rebuked Diana in the way she wrote to the Duchess of York in March 1995, when she thundered: 'Clearly you have never considered the damage you are causing us all. How dare you discredit us like this. You have done more to bring shame on the family than could ever have been imagined.'

Other Royals were exasperated by Diana's behaviour and might well have written to her in this vein, though they didn't – Prince Philip and Princess Anne, for example.

Philip was positively brusque towards Diana on a number of occasions and the Princess revealed to her friends, including Roberto Devorik, that her father-in-law considered her to be 'an idiot'. And yet in his letters to her, Philip (whom Diana always talked of as 'the real head of the family') often tried to be constructive.

Princess Anne's attitude to Diana was one of indifference. They never went out of their way to meet. Although Diana admired Anne's strength of character, the Princess Royal would have been one of the last people she would have called to talk over a problem.

Prince Andrew – the one Diana had considered 'so good-looking' as a child when they were growing up as neighbours in Norfolk – was the Royal with whom she got on best. She identified with him because she felt that, just like herself, he was underrated by the rest of the Royals, 'squashed' by them, as she put it, and, like her, 'dismissed as an idiot'.

Andrew was often there on those lonely Sundays after both their separations when Diana would drive over to Fergie's home for lunch. He would never say a word against his older brother, but Diana sensed from the unfailingly good-natured way he treated her, with lots of banter and jokes that they both enjoyed, that he was a secret ally or, at the least, someone who understood.

Diana felt that Prince Edward tended to avoid her. She knew he thought she had let the side down, though he went out of his way to avoid a face-to-face confrontation. He believed, quite wrongly, that Diana was responsible for leaking to the media details of the Queen's 70th birthday party in 1996, which was cancelled as a result. But he never accused her of it directly.

Diana's relationship with the Queen Mother was never easy to plumb. In her taped 'Squidgy' phone conversation with James Gilbey, she talked of the 'strange look' she noticed the Queen Mother giving her over lunch: 'It's not hatred, it's sort of interest and pity.'

She came to feel that the Queen Mother, an iron disciplinarian in matters of royal discretion, had bracketed Diana with her mother, Frances, who had been disloyal to her husband.

The Queen, of course, was a pivotal figure in the Princess's life. Hers was the signature at the bottom of letters she had sent urging Charles and Diana to get on with settling the divorce negotiations which she feared were damaging the monarchy.

The correspondence was a direct consequence of Diana's *Panorama* interview in November 1995 and was a rare intervention by the Queen in her heir's domestic affairs. How Diana wished that her mother-in-law had intervened more frequently and positively.

The Princess felt that the Queen privately sympathized with her, but believed she was too accepting of the fact that Charles had a mistress, turning a blind eye instead of doing something about it. Naïvely, perhaps, she wished the Queen had taken her son to one side and told him that he could not have both a wife and mistress.

During the separation, Diana and the Queen would occasionally have tea, usually with William and Harry. After the divorce, their meetings were not discontinued, but were certainly fewer.

Diana had a brief friendship with her Kensington Palace neighbour Princess Michael of Kent, even though they could not have been more different. When, deep into their own troubled marriages, Diana and Fergie realized that the Royal Family loathed the haughty, Austrian-born Marie-Christine, they decided to befriend her. They made a point of defending her whenever her name was mentioned.

Both ruefully reflected later that, of the three of them, only 'Princess Pushy' had kept the title HRH.

Leaving Buckingham Palace on the day after her separation was announced in December 1992. Diana knew there could be no turning back.

Chapter 10

THE INDEPENDENT PRINCESS

One day in 1996 in the LA Fitness Centre at Isleworth, Middlesex, the Princess and a friend were talking, as women do, about bust sizes. The friend said to Diana: 'Well, you don't have to worry, you've got a great chest.' Diana gave her an old-fashioned look and replied: 'Yes, but you should see my husband's lady.'

This quip is evidence that Diana was changing. It was three years since she had begun seriously working out and her bulimia was coming under control. She was still a long way from that statuesque shape which was to give her a commanding presence in any circumstances and the confidence of which she had always thought herself incapable. But she was moving in that direction.

She had started gentle exercises in 1989, not intending to reshape her body but to occupy her troubled mind. She also hoped it would raise her energy levels and stop her feeling so tired.

Her diary was full of engagements that brought out adoring crowds in thousands, yet she dreaded fulfilling them. According to her first trainer, Carolan Brown, Diana was like a young girl who had been suppressed and not allowed to develop her character.

'She would weep and say she couldn't face shaking hands for another day,' Carolan recalls. 'She didn't feel like putting on glamorous clothes and going out. She wanted to stay at home in her tracksuit.'

Diana would exercise at her Kensington Palace apartment in a sitting room full of family photos and antiques. Her then butler, Harold Brown, would push back the sofas so she could work out.

Carolan had seen the Princess on television looking wonderful at engagements and was consequently surprised to discover that she was completely lacking in confidence and self-esteem. The reality behind the glamour of the world's most photographed woman was

(Opposite): *All the energy Diana had used in trying to save her marriage was now thrown into her fitness regime. Here, she is seen leaving the Chelsea Harbour Club in 1996.*
(Above): *A wet Princess after a Pavarotti concert in Hyde Park in July 1991.*

that she was terribly anxious and was always asking: 'Do I look all right?'

Friends had come to realize that she felt so unloved and discarded that she needed the boost of compliments and constant reassurance. Diana was always being described as beautiful, but she did not believe she really was and such comments would embarrass her.

Now here she was doing exercises that would in time, and with the advice of former England rugby captain Will Carling, get close to body-building.

At first, Diana couldn't understand why she had begun to feel so much better. The exercises were helping, but nothing much had changed in her life. The answer was that her downcast eyes (which everyone had noticed when she was a child) were accentuated by her tendency, at almost 5ft 11in, to stoop. Because she felt scrutinized in public, the stoop had become a positive slump.

Carolan's first task was to work on Diana's posture, teaching her to sit up straight, pull up her head and look ahead. This also had the effect of pulling in her stomach, the part of her body about which she was most self-conscious.

It was quite a revelation to the royal household when she started wearing a thong leotard around her apartment, which embarrassed her butler. One friend recalls that the Princess liked to come to the door of her apartment in her leotard to say goodbye 'so the policemen could see her. She loved teasing them'. When Diana started going to the gym, she would always wear mascara. It wasn't that she was vain. She felt that looking good was part of her role as Princess of Wales. But the change in her self-esteem came too late: the marriage breakdown had become unstoppable.

In a curious way, Diana even managed to draw a new strength from this failure. When John Major announced the separation in the House of Commons on 9 December 1992, she reasoned that at least she no longer had to devote precious energy to trying to keep the marriage together.

How ironic that this was to be the trigger for her to complete her metamorphosis from despairing Princess to confident new woman. She had already begun receiving tuition in speech-making from the former

Stunning, and with all the confidence of a woman in control of her life again: Diana at a charity concert in Modena, Italy, 1995.

Charles and Diana at the Royal Variety Performance in December 1992.
It was their last engagement together before their separation.

Coronation Street actor Peter Settelen (he was introduced to her by Carolan Brown) and these intensified. In less than a year, she had sixty sessions with him.

By 1993, when she made her 'time and space' speech (in which she announced her decision to drastically cut down on her public engagements), she was beginning to sound, look and, crucially, feel like a new woman.

Diana was aware that, thanks to fitness training up to three times a week, her body had taken on a new, womanly shape. The bulimia had been all but driven out.

By 1995, the Princess had established herself as a major international figure. Her voice was strong and her shoulders were straighter and newly broadened by the physical regime she had set herself.

The Parker Bowles's marriage was dissolved in January 1995. Diana's marriage to the Prince of Wales ended, after

fifteen years, on 28 August 1996. Now there was a steely look in Diana's famous blue eyes. She had her own life to lead. Even Camilla didn't trouble her any more.

The moment that the Princess of Wales stopped thinking like one of life's victims and began to be an independent woman happened as she watched her belongings arrive at Kensington Palace from Highgrove and Prince Charles's being carted off in the opposite direction. It was December 1992 and they were separating. 'It makes me feel so sad and empty,' Diana said.

But later, after Charles had called to collect his personal effects, she did something totally unexpected. She giggled and said to a close friend: 'My husband has cleaned the place out. I'm surprised he didn't take the light switches.'

To Diana's friends, that giggle, last heard when she was being romanced by James Hewitt, was the signal of a new beginning. Someone quite different, and very determined, was replacing the bulimia-racked, uncertain woman who had become a Princess eleven years earlier. It also marked the start of a remarkable new relationship with her husband as Diana began to win back his high regard.

In the summer of 1996, the Princess came bounding up to Jenni Rivett, chortling: 'My husband's up to something: he's just told me I've got nice legs.' Diana had been surprised, and flattered, for it had been a long time since Charles had paid her a compliment. It made her, says Jenni, 'girlishly happy'.

But then, Charles knew that Diana had begun to say nice things about him, and even to him in person. Simone Simmons recalls how the Princess had a fit of the giggles at William's Eton carol concert in December 1996 when Charles turned up wearing a pair of shiny brown shoes. She told him he looked like Fred Astaire. That was the cheeky Diana he had first met when she was sixteen. As then, they laughed together.

James Hewitt and Diana at Combermere Barracks, Windsor, where he was helping her to overcome her fear of horses. It was 1989 and the height of their affair.

It was a nostalgic sound, their laughter, which at one stage neither had imagined the other would ever hear again and which Diana had always believed could never be quite the same with the Prince's mistress, Camilla Parker Bowles.

They had only recently emerged from a dark period of implacable enmity in which each had deliberately set out to undermine the other. Their friends had become their armies in what was known as the War of the Waleses, and which we shall return to in a later chapter of our story.

Now divorced, Diana's anger at Charles's behaviour during their marriage had largely subsided and she was working towards an amicable relationship with the father of her sons.

Charles, however, could not have failed to notice that other men had been paying copious compliments to his former wife. This was exactly what she wanted him to see.

She was keen to demonstrate the differences between herself and the older, less glamorous Camilla, though the suggestions that she dreamed that she and Charles might be reconciled are wide of the mark. She knew there was no turning back.

And the Princess had, as she privately admitted to a friend, a 'vengeful streak'. (She would gleefully tell the story of how, when she was a teenager, a friend had refused to lend her his car, so she put glue in the driver's door lock.)

There was undoubtedly an element of something close to vengeance in her *Panorama* interview in

November 1995, though it had not started out that way. Diana's intention was to put her case as frankly as Charles had put his, eighteen months previously, in his television interview with Jonathan Dimbleby.

Privately she explained that, although she had shown that she could lead an independent life, she felt justified in telling her side of the story and relating her 'suffering and disillusionment'. She told Roberto Devorik: 'It would be hypocritical for me to complain if I do not tell the truth about myself. I can't present myself as a saint because I'm not a saint.'

It was for this reason that she admitted, for the first and only time, having an affair with James Hewitt. Her memorable words were that she 'adored him... I was in love with him'.

But was this really the case? Many of her friends believe she deliberately said she loved Hewitt to get back at her husband for his infidelity. Their view is that although Diana was infatuated for a time with the handsome officer, she was never in love with him.

When the affair began in the late Eighties, she had been very lonely and Hewitt had helped to fill her empty marriage. As a close woman friend explains: 'The truth is that she didn't feel for Hewitt anything like the total love that she felt for her husband.'

The Princess confided to Devorik, among others, that Hewitt was not the love of her life. 'He was simply, if you like, a visa in her passport that gave her a first exploration of life outside marriage', he says.

The men friends: With Gulu Lalvani (top),
Will Carling (left), *Teddy Forstmann* (above right)
and Dr Hasnat Khan (above left).

Diana had become the epitome of a modern, independent woman of the Nineties, whether working out at the Chelsea Harbour Club (opposite) or by wearing head-turning outfits such as this dress (above) on a visit to London's Hale Clinic.

Her feelings for Hewitt were to turn to contempt when he subsequently gave his unfettered support to a *roman-à-clef*, the cloyingly written *Princess In Love*, based on their relationship.

Her affair with Hewitt, of course, pre-dated the new, independent Diana. And when he phoned her out of the blue to offer his commiserations on the day that she and Charles were divorced, 28 August 1996, the Princess was well able to deal with him.

She hesitated before picking up the phone, perhaps because in one of the lower floor lavatories in her Kensington Palace apartment she had hung a cartoon depicting a pile of manure swarming with flies and captioned: 'What's that smell? Must be James Hewitt.'

When she took the call, Hewitt told her he was sorry about the divorce and wished her every happiness in the future.

Diana had read in the newspapers that he had bought a house with the proceeds of that book so she used the opportunity to take him to task. 'I see you've got a new home,' she said pointedly, adding later to a friend '... a house that I effectively helped pay for.' Of course by this time, Hewitt's was not the only name to which she had been linked. Diana had a number of men friends (ranging from billionaire Teddy Forstmann and England rugby star Will Carling to Asian businessman Gulu Lalvani and heart surgeon Hasnat Khan) with whom, inevitably for a woman whose marriage had been so unhappy, she was variously described as being 'in love'.

One reason for this was her habit of visiting them in their homes or inviting them to her Kensington Palace apartment. These visits gave rise to a hubbub of gossip and speculation. But was it really 'your place or mine' or something else altogether? Diana's explanation puts it in a very different and understandable light.

'I can go to any smart restaurant I like and be wined and dined any night of the week,' she said. 'But what I really love is going to a man's home. It allows me to be normal.'

The image of a discarded wife hungry for love is only partly true. Diana was certainly being flirtatious and allowing herself to be courted. It was important to her to be sexually desired, but friends knew she preferred attention rather than a full-blown affair.

'The trouble is that these men would fall in love with her,' says her long-time friend, the beautician Janet

Filderman. It has been suggested that Diana did not mind publicity about the men in her life, that she liked the notoriety of being linked with them because of all the times she had been rejected, starting with her parents' separation when she was five and ending with her husband seeking out the company of a less attractive woman.

The truth is that she feared gossip because of the effect it could have on her sons William and Harry and her fears that it could damage the divorce negotiations. And, as she told her friend Richard Greene, an American businessman: 'Romance is overstated. What I'm looking for is a lifelong friend.'

Though accomplished in the art of flirting, Diana was initially naïve when it came to dating. She was put in a quandary when a man she had met, and liked, phoned her one evening. She was putting Harry to bed and couldn't take the call. 'Shall I call him or shall I wait until he calls me again?' she asked a good friend. 'I wonder whether he thought I deliberately didn't take his call.'

Yet men friends were the standard bearers of her new independence. And why not, since she was virtually unattached? No efforts were being made to conceal Charles's affair, although he took care never to be seen with Camilla.

She became friends with the then England rugby captain Will Carling, whom she met while working out at the Chelsea Harbour Club and whose marriage was virtually over within a year after his wedding. Diana was flattered by the interest Carling showed in her. It might never have happened if she hadn't gone up to him as he did sit-ups and joked: 'You don't know how to work your abdominals properly.' This was the beginning of the friendship over which Diana's critics were to accuse her of being a home wrecker. Angrily, she denied it.

She and Carling met often, sometimes at the club and sometimes at Kensington Palace. Eventually, his wife, the television presenter Julia Carling, hinted that she had put her foot down: her husband's meetings with the Princess had to stop. The implications of this news were barely absorbed before Carling's dark blue Range Rover was seen in the Palace car park. He had called to give England rugby shirts to William and Harry – Diana was out at the time. Julia spat fire. Diana, she said, had 'picked the wrong couple,' adding:

'It would be easy to say she's ruined my marriage. But it takes two to tango and I blame Will for getting involved in the first place.'

The Carlings parted in September 1995 and Diana was not involved in their divorce the following year. For her part, the Princess always maintained that the Carlings's marital difficulties were a matter for them.

Other friendships were also troubled. Many of Diana's circle believed she was looking for a father figure in such men as the 53-year-old married art dealer Oliver Hoare. Old Etonian Hoare, a dashing figure and a good friend of the Prince of Wales, and his wife, the French oil heiress Diane de Waldner, had been guests at a Royal Ascot house party at Windsor Castle in the Eighties and by the early Nineties Oliver and the Princess had become close friends.

It was Mrs Hoare who called in the police in 1994 after taking a number of silent nuisance calls at their Chelsea home… some of which were traced to one of the Princess's private lines at Kensington Palace. The Metropolitan Police Commissioner Sir Paul Condon announced that the inquiries had been ended 'at Mr Hoare's request'. The suggestion was that some, but not all, of the calls had been made by the Princess herself.

Teddy Forstmann, the 57-year-old billionaire American financier and head of Gulfstream, the aviation company, was typical of the powerful new friends of both sexes that Diana was making, especially in the United States.

He used one of his jets to fly Diana around the U.S. and introduced her to new friends, such as the newspaper publisher Kay Graham and the U.S. President's wife, Hillary Clinton. Ill-informed commentators couldn't resist suggesting a romance with Forstmann, but their relationship was strictly platonic and they shared much laughter. Diana was an entertaining mimic of his racy accent, especially when recounting the phone call in which he asked whether her boys liked bubble gum. When she said 'Yes', he replied: 'That's great, 'cos I own

a bubble gum factory.' Then he asked whether her boys liked baseball. Again, she said 'Yes'. 'Well, that's great, too,' he replied, 'because I own a baseball stadium.'

The Princess knew that people like Forstmann were criticized, and even derided, by court circles, but he was helping her back into the world after she had endured more than a decade of the restricted life of a Royal.

She told the Asian tycoon Gulu Lalvani, who became a friend through charity work, that she loved 'having the freedom to enjoy myself in a public place'.

If there was one man friend who genuinely stirred her emotionally, it was the 38-year-old Pakistani heart surgeon, Dr Hasnat Khan, who works under Professor Sir Magdi Yacoub at London's Royal Brompton Hospital.

She visited his family in Lahore when she was in Pakistan seeing her old friend Jemima Khan (James Goldsmith's daughter who had married the former cricketer Imran Khan) and entertained them to tea at Kensington Palace. After years spent in the company of well-bred Englishmen who had little to do of any importance, she welcomed the handsome doctor's commitment to her yearning to help people, by using his 'healing hands'.

Diana and Hasnat were very close, but his father, Rasheed, insists that they were 'good and loyal friends and nothing more. They did not have an affair and there was no question of marriage. It is not necessary that two good friends should marry'.

One of the most powerful images of Diana's caring nature arrived in a letter to Dr Khan's parents after there had been an embarrassing amount of publicity about her friendship with their son. The Princess wrote to say how sorry she was that their lives had been disturbed by the speculation. But the hand-written line they remember most said simply: 'Without love, people die.'

Sunbathing at a polo match at Windsor, May 1992. At last, Diana felt that she could throw off the shackles of royal protocol and be herself.

Chapter 11

A WOMAN OF STATURE

The change that had come in the newly independent Diana's life was, in many respects, almost as big as the makeover that had taken place when she became the Princess of Wales. Not only was she learning about men for the first time in her life, but she was also working hard to turn herself into a practised public speaker.

Camilla Parker Bowles had ceased to be of significance in her life, because the Princess no longer had Charles to share with her. Diana believed there was no prospect that Camilla could ever be seen in public with the Prince and that Mrs Parker Bowles would play no part in the upbringing of William and Harry. An unspoken agreement between the Prince and the Princess meant that whenever Charles had the boys at Highgrove, Camilla, who spent so much time there, was never around.

Indeed, early in the separation Diana began to feel almost sorry for Mrs Parker Bowles, for she knew at least where she was going and she realized that Camilla had no idea what the future held.

Meanwhile, Diana had a new life to live and she was determined to make a success of it. Under the guidance of Peter Settelen, Diana spent night after night reading old Mariella Frostrup scripts from television's *The Little Picture Show* off an autocue. She got to be quite good at it.

At the same time, commercial offers worth millions of pounds began to arrive on her desk and, surprisingly, she did consider them. An Italian fashion designer offered her £1 million to appear on the catwalk in one of his outfits. The Princess canvassed friends before deciding not to do it.

In December 1996, a woman's magazine invited her to be consultant editor of a special issue, as Hillary Clinton had done in America, and again she asked around before reluctantly turning it down.

Likewise with Kevin Costner's suggestion that she could star in a remake of *The Bodyguard*. She never took this idea entirely seriously but said: 'Wouldn't it be fabulous to go to my own premiere?'

(Opposite): *At last free from her husband, Diana knew exactly where she was going, which was more than could be said for Charles's mistress, Camilla (above).*

On a skiing holiday with her long-time friends Catherine Soames (left)
and Kate Menzies (centre) *at Lech, Austria, March 1994.*
Both would soon find themselves frozen out of Diana's circle.

She asked one friend how much money she could expect from such a deal and, when she was told it could be worth £10 million, Diana said: 'Wow, think of the holidays we could have.'

One of the most intriguing commercial ventures, and one which might well have happened, was the secret plan to create a perfume in her name to raise money for a planned new charity, Children of the World. Diana suggested that the ingredients should come from all the different countries in which she had worked. The bottle would be in the shape of a D for Diana.

But for the divorce and the negotiations which preceded it, the perfume might well have been on sale now. But, to the Princess's dismay, the project was vetoed by the small print of the divorce deal which prevented her from being involved in commercial undertakings. This was a rare reversal for the newly independent Diana. Elsewhere, she had managed to control the direction of her life to a spectacular degree.

There was almost an air of defiance about the Princess which her friend Gulu Lalvani believes was the result of her being toughened by the 'shock of her divorce'. Diana was, he says, 'strong, independent and positively-minded,

a woman who was enjoying the freedom of carving a new role.'

He recalled: 'We had dinner at Harry's Bar in Mayfair and afterwards she said she'd like to go dancing at Annabel's. She hadn't been there for eleven or twelve years, since she and Fergie had dressed up as policewomen on Prince Andrew's stag night. She pulled me on to the dance floor whenever a song appealed to her. She was a very good dancer and we stayed there from 11pm until 2am. She loved doing ordinary things like that.'

Despite being marginalized from royal life by Buckingham Palace, Diana had become an international figure of stature. Through her land mines campaign, she had even achieved the unofficial ambassador status she had always wanted.

She had set out to become a power player with friends in every continent and had succeeded beyond even her own expectations. At this level among international high-fliers, she no longer felt the need to sift people into piles of friends or foes. Nor was there any need to let people get too close, which tended to make her feel exposed and vulnerable.

Baroness Chalker, the former Minister for Overseas Development, noted the metamorphosis of Diana from

After years of hiding her bulimia-stricken body, Diana delighted in showing off her
womanly curves on holiday on the Caribbean island of Nevis in January 1993.

the shy figure she had met in 1985 (when the Princess had talked of her worries about the safety of small children in cars) to, a decade later, a woman determined to succeed who had become 'incredibly skilled at persuading people that things have to change'.

There was a new, easy confidence about the Princess, even with tough intellects such as the Baroness. In 1993 when the minister went to Nepal on the Princess's first solo visit after her separation from Charles, the Baroness was 'not looking my best.' Diana instantly offered her the services of her personal hairdresser.

In the years after her separation, the Princess had moved from uncertainty to being resolute and, in many respects, implacable in her independence. Against

security advice, she had, at the end of 1993, even insisted on shedding her police bodyguards.

She had assumed a completely private style of life which was totally foreign to other women in the Royal Family. Although Camilla no longer troubled her, Diana was honest enough to admit to a certain satisfaction in knowing that her own independence was now greater than Camilla's.

Her new independence had become a highly prized personal possession. This was especially so in her friendships. The new Diana conducted them on her own terms and at her own cautious pace. An acquaintance couldn't make the first move towards her at a party. The trick was to let her find them.

Those long hours reciting television scripts had paid off. The articulate Diana, addressing a fashion awards gala in New York in January 1995, had come a long way from the diffident Princess.

Tiresome though this may have been, it was important to Diana because of the years she had endured as Princess of Wales seldom knowing who were her real friends and who were the social climbers. But she set impossibly unrealistic targets in what she expected from her friends and so the turnover in her circle was high.

Two of the casualties were Catherine Soames, the former wife of the Tory MP Nicholas, and the heiress Kate Menzies, who had accompanied the Princess on skiing trips and Caribbean holidays as well as long lunches in fashionable London restaurants and nights out at the cinema.

Both were frozen out of Diana's trusted inner circle during 1995. The Princess did not attend Kate's marriage to restaurateur Simon Slater in February 1996 because she was on a charity visit to Pakistan. She would not have wanted to turn her friend's wedding into a media circus anyway, but some saw her non-attendance as a snub. Their falling out baffled Kate and Catherine, as it had baffled others. No one could ever plumb what precisely Diana was looking for in her friendships. One clue may be that behind the new independence, the old, uncertain Diana, easily wounded, ever afraid of betrayal or becoming too dependent on another, had not completely gone. She would sometimes arrive at the Marylebone consulting rooms of osteopath Michael Skipwith in tears because a friend she 'thought she could trust' had let her down.

The Princess had suffered with back problems from childhood after falling from a horse. She got to know Skipwith's other patients as she waited, like them, for her turn. She used to help one particular little girl do her homework in the waiting room while her mother was being treated upstairs.

For the first few months of her visits, American-born Skipwith addressed the Princess as 'Ma'am'. Then one day she said: 'For goodness sake, Michael, you see me without my clothes. Just call me Diana.' (Contrary to popular opinion, the Princess was very comfortable with her body, much more so than most women he treated. She would take her clothes off in a very relaxed way.)

But despite her new independence, Diana was still hyper-sensitive, reacting severely, sometimes unfairly, to anything that smacked of disloyalty. Nothing illustrates this with greater clarity than her relationship with her sister-in-law and one-time best friend, the Duchess of York. It is widely known that Fergie upset Diana in her autobiography by light-heartedly recording that she had contracted verrucas after borrowing a pair of Diana's shoes. The book came out just a few weeks after the two women had returned from a joint holiday with their children in the South of France.

The effect of Fergie's book on their relationship was, as their mutual friend, the Hong Kong millionaire David Tang, calls it: 'An arctic freeze.' The Princess would not even allow Fergie's name to be mentioned in her company.

Yet they had once been inseparable. Right from the beginning they had been allies and friends: both were outsiders brought into the Royal Family who had found it hard to do things right. They leaned on each for support, they consulted, they even plotted – there was that famous agreement to leave their husbands simultaneously which never came about.

When eventually both were living separated lives, Fergie's home Romenda Lodge became the refuge to which Diana retreated as often as she could, usually on Sundays for lunch and, whenever possible, with her sons. The two women were so close that Diana had become almost a second mother to Fergie's daughters Beatrice and Eugenie. And suddenly: nothing. Just a social vacuum between the accident-prone Duchess and the over-sensitive Princess.

In fact, Diana was outraged by more than just Fergie's mention of shoes and verrucas, although she felt the usual symptoms of betrayal. She also blamed Fergie's post-divorce financial activities for making her own divorce negotiations with the Royal Family more difficult.

Nine months after the freeze began, Tang attempted to bring about a reconciliation. He arranged a dinner party for the Princess at Mark's Club, the Mayfair dining spot run by Mark Birley. He followed his usual practice of letting Diana know whom he was proposing would join them – Fergie. When he telephoned Kensington Palace to confirm arrangements, the message from the Princess was unequivocal: 'The Duchess of York is the one person who would not be welcome.'

In time there is no doubt that, having been through so much together, a rapprochement would surely have come. Sadly, there wasn't enough time. Two months later, Diana was dead.

Chapter 12

FASHION ICON

Leah Gottlieb, the founder, owner and designer of the Gottex swimwear company, is in her 70s. But when the manageress of her West End showroom told her that the Princess of Wales had made an appointment in the summer of 1997 to choose a few things for a holiday in the South of France, she did not hesitate. Within minutes of hanging up the phone, Leah was booked on a plane from her home in Tel Aviv to London.

Diana was touched that Miss Gottlieb had made such an effort. As the fashion designer Roland Klein says: 'Diana knew her power. She was completely aware of the impact of her looks and position, and she used it. But she never took people's response to her for granted.'

When she had chosen her swimsuits (including the sexy leopard print one-piece pictured here, which said so much about her mood in those final days in St Tropez in the summer of 1997) and chatted about fashion and family, Diana rose to leave. Then, with a mischievous grin, she asked the shop manageress, Pauline Lewis, where her camera was.

Everywhere she went, everyone wanted a picture of the Princess, and Pauline was no exception. Flustered, the manageress admitted that her camera was on her desk, loaded with film and ready to go. She had intended to ask the Princess's permission to take a photograph as a memento of the royal visit but had lost her nerve.

'Well, fetch it,' said Diana in tones of mock command. When the flash failed to go off, Pauline was deeply disappointed.

'Never mind,' said Diana, 'if nothing comes out, I can always come back next week.' And, with hugs all round, she was off to play in the sun with her beloved boys and to fall in love.

It had been a long journey from those days back in late 1980 when the fashion industry first became aware of Lady Diana Spencer. Then they had clucked over the perfidiousness of the photographers who had manoeuvred the pretty teenager into standing with the light behind her so that her long legs were clearly discernible through the flimsy cotton of her Laura Ashley skirt and, famously, over her own lack of sophistication when she had emerged from a car at her first official evening engagement, literally spilling out of her ill-fitting low-cut gown.

Her clothes told you so much about the 19-year-old in love with the Prince of Wales. As expected from a daughter

(Opposite): *This stunning photograph was taken by Diana's favourite photographer, Patrick Demarchelier.*
(Above): *Diana in a leopard print one-piece swimsuit on holiday in St Tropez.*

of the British aristocracy, by day she wore the unimaginative and frumpy uniform of the Sloane Ranger.

Upper-class girls of limited education and less ambition filled in the time between finishing school and a good marriage sharing London mansion flats and doing undemanding little jobs with children, in art galleries or on the fringes of the fashion world, all within a mile of Sloane Square.

A Sloane's wardrobe consisted of print or corduroy skirts, pie-crust frilled blouses, a single string of modest-sized pearls, a basic crew-neck or V-neck jumper and flat shoes, usually black patent leather with a little grosgrain bow.

Diana was a classic example of the genre. On the day she got engaged, 24 February 1981, she recalled: 'I had one long dress, one silk shirt, one smart pair of shoes and that was it. Suddenly my mother and I had to buy six of everything.

'We bought as much as we thought we needed but we still didn't have enough. Bear in mind that when you have to change four times a day, suddenly your wardrobe has to expand unbelievably.'

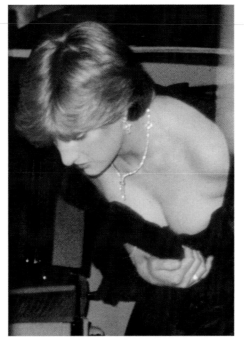

Diana in the Emanuel gown she wore to her first evening occasion after the engagement, a dress that provoked much less-than-flattering comment.

Diana's mother, Frances Shand Kydd, introduced her newly engaged daughter to her first fashion designer, Caroline Charles. She is one of the few designers who retains the respect of the fashion Press, with its preoccupation with novelty, while satisfying the country set's preference for the conservative and conventional.

'Diana was a joy to dress because she was tall and everything sat well on her,' says Caroline. 'But what impressed me was how thoughtful she was. I remember her choosing a velvet suit for a visit to the blind because they would enjoy touching it.

'And we would experiment with necklines so that modesty would be maintained when she leaned forward.' However, Diana's first formal outfit was a panic buy from Harrods. Her mother helped her choose the blue Cojana suit in which she posed for her engagement pictures with Prince Charles. Neither Frances, living a country life, nor her youngest daughter knew anything about fashion. While the suit was a provincial mother's idea of something smart and grown-up, it looked gauchely middle-aged on a young woman with a baby face and long athletic limbs.

The two older Spencer girls, Jane and Sarah, had worked briefly at *Vogue*. They knew their little sister needed expert help so they introduced her to *Vogue*'s editor, Beatrix Miller, who called in Anna Harvey, the magazine's fashion editor. Anna was not only au fait with royal ways and the demands of a formal lifestyle, but she was also gentle and discreet.

For her first meeting with the newly engaged Diana, Anna called all the designers she thought might be appropriate and asked them to send samples to *Vogue*'s offices in Hanover Square.

She ordered far too many clothes because, as she later said: 'I had absolutely no idea of the kind of thing Diana liked. By the time she arrived, I was shaking like a leaf.

'But I took one look at her and thought: "This isn't going to be too difficult after all." She was about 5ft 10in and completely in proportion. Her eyes lit up when she saw all the racks – I don't think she had any idea how many lovely things there were out there – and her enthusiasm was contagious.'

The meetings before the wedding were held in the editor's office: Beatrix Miller would be ousted. After the marriage, Anna Harvey would 'trundle over to Kensington Palace with a rail of clothes for Diana to go through. We'd sit on the floor in her drawing room, looking at sketches and swatches of fabric, while the butler brought endless cups of coffee'.

David and Elizabeth Emanuel were among the first designers Anna introduced to Diana. High romance

Putting more formal dressing behind her at the Christie's auction, June 1997, in Catherine Walker's completely modern, beaded pastel floral-patterned short sheath.

One step ahead of the fashion pack in Walker's gilt and glitter number for the ballet, March 1996.

One aspect of royal life over the years which amazed Diana was the number of times a day she had to change her clothes, an exercise which she, rather irritably, regarded as archaic. She was expected to wear everything from short cocktail dresses through dinner, opera and theatre dresses of varying degrees of formality to full-blown, state-occasion ballgowns. Diana loved cocktail dresses because they felt young and modern, and showed off her long, shapely legs. She usually chose a starkly simple sheath, preferably bare-armed and cleavage-enhancing, by Catherine Walker, Jacques Azagury, Tomasz Starzewski, Gianni Versace and Christian Lacroix.

The ultimate look-at-me satin-topped little dress by Christian Lacroix at the Petit Palais, Paris, 1995.

Diana's love of Hollywood glamour earned disapproval from Buckingham Palace, but she dazzled the stars at 1983's Octopussy premiere in Hachi's beaded gown.

'One never quite understood the Princess's passion for the one-sleeved dress,' said her fashion adviser Anna Harvey of *Vogue* with indulgent affection. Especially when the one sleeve was topped with a *Dynasty*-style shoulder pad. But Diana did like asymmetry and demanded it from her designers whether or not it was fashionable. Even at the height of her bulimia in the early Eighties, she occasionally abandoned her habit of covering up her wasted body to wear one-sleeved dresses, even though they exposed her thin shoulders. Thanks to her exercise regime in the Nineties, the Princess's body became more athletic. Her best features were her limbs and fine bosom so, when the occasion dictated a full-length gown, she liked to show off at least one well-muscled arm.

Diana liked the teasing element of one proper side and one naughtily bare. She was, after all, a flirt who was mischievously aware of her power to enchant.

A simple silk sheath by Versace for a 1996 party in Sydney typified her mature style: pared-down and sleek.

Catherine Walker's damask sheath was a perfect choice for a film premiere in 1991.

(frills, flounces and *Gone With The Wind* crinolines) was the fashion in the early Eighties and the Emanuels were very much the designers of the moment. Diana chose them to make her wedding dress.

'She was such a romantic figure and we told her we would make her a fairy-tale dress,' says David Emanuel.

They went through pictures of all the previous royal wedding dresses and decided, says Elizabeth Emanuel, that 'we had to outdo them all. Diana had such a sense of humour and she was so funny about it. We found out which royal dress had the longest train – I think it was Queen Mary's – and then we said: 'OK, it's got to be longer than that!'

The off-the-shoulder dress Diana wore for her first formal evening occasion after the engagement, and which attracted so much criticism, was one she had seen that day on a rail in the Emanuels' showroom. 'I was so excited,' Diana remembered. 'A black dress from the Emanuels! I thought it was OK because girls my age would wear this dress. I had not appreciated that I was seen as a royal lady, although I'd only got one ring on my finger as opposed to two rings. Black to me was the smartest colour you could possibly have at the age of nineteen. It was a real grown-up dress. I was quite big-chested then and they all got frightfully excited... it was a horrendous occasion.'

The problem was that the dress was not made to measure. It slipped too low and appeared, according to some pictures, to show a lot more than it should. A censorious Press went overboard. Prudence Glynn of *The Times* said Diana 'looked as if she was sitting in a hip bath'.

It was a traumatic experience for the teenager. And a precedent had been set. No other royal woman had been so evaluated on her appearance. Princess Marina, the Greek princess who had married the Duke of Kent in the Thirties, had been judged chic but the other frumpier royals had set themselves outside fashion.

Now, with the gauntlet thrown down by the fashion Press, Diana's need to look stunning was to become a compulsion, perhaps born of her insecurity and a child-like need for approval.

But if admiration was the primary objective of Diana the mannequin, it was not the only one. She learned to use clothes as a language, as a way of signalling what she was feeling to an insatiably interested world.

She was a butterfly who went through several metamorphoses, reinventing herself with great courage and extraordinary resilience.

Despite the underlying theme of self-destruction which shaped the early years of her marriage, Diana's appearance told us of her iron will to survive and of her impressive resourcefulness.

She loved the sense of power that clothes could give her. She soon discovered that a frock could become a weapon to blast her estranged husband off the front pages, as she so elegantly proved in that little cocktail number by Christina Stambolian which she wore to the Serpentine Gallery in June 1995. It was the night that Prince Charles admitted in his interview with Jonathan Dimbleby that he had committed adultery with Camilla Parker Bowles.

In the language of clothes, that dress said many things. Black for mourning, black for sophistication, black for mature sexuality. It revealed shoulders and thigh. It rejected the conventions of royal dress and declared Diana's independence. And it asserted the beauty of its wearer. But Diana also knew that her beauty could be a handicap, blinding the puritanical to that part of her which felt more comfortable with sick and disadvantaged people.

Reflecting on some of the last pictures of the Princess taken during her field trips to promote the campaign against land mines, the fashion designer Bruce Oldfield thinks that the clotheshorse image was a diversion which, while it may have become a pleasure, was certainly not the real Diana.

He said: 'She committed herself to looking good because it was a way of doing her job well and she very quickly became certain about what she wanted to achieve. And if you offered a contradictory thought, she could even be a bit petulant. But when she was pleased, she showed it.'

Certainly, Diana always received warmth, admiration and help from the fashion world. The Princess felt at ease among fashion people because of their lack of reserve and their willingness to express affection and admiration openly and physically. She loved to do photographic shoots, not just because the results confirmed her attractiveness (she was always bewildered that people considered her beautiful) but also because they were a chance to enter, if just for a day, a cocoon of unstinted affection, admiration and bonding.

'We were all protective,' says Freddie Fox, her milliner from the mid-Eighties until her separation from Charles in December 1992 when her more informal lifestyle meant that she no longer needed to wear hats.

'We wanted her to feel good and look good. We know how much the former depends on the latter. She made a lot of mistakes in the beginning. Some early outfits were more like fancy dress. In particular I remember a drum majorette outfit she wore to some military do. She thought she was paying her hosts a compliment, having some fun, but it went down badly. But she learned.' And what she learned, she used.

Harold King, founder-director of the London City Ballet, remembers Diana asking him if she could come to a greyhound racing evening to raise funds for the ballet. She arrived in a black tuxedo with a green waistcoat. 'It was a clever move. She knew we needed the publicity and, sure enough, she got her picture and a mention of the ballet on the front pages the next morning,' he says. 'She later said to me: "You know I'm a good fund-raising tool so make sure you invite me to these things."'

Making a grand entrance in Versace during her visit to Chicago in June 1996. By this time, Diana had established her personal style: sophisticated, sexy and, above all, modern.

Certainly, the Diana of the last couple of years was confident in her taste. The auction in New York which cleared her wardrobe of some of her grandest gowns was more than a space-making exercise. It was truly a case of off with the old, on with the new.

Her evening wear was revealingly body-hugging and minimalist. For many fashion commentators, the purple Versace gown she wore on her visit to Chicago in June 1996 summed up the new Diana: dashing and sexy, young and modern, confident and finally at ease with her body.

It reflected the attitude expressed on her last visit to the French designer Roland Klein when she examined her hemline in the mirror and urged: 'Shorter, shorter.' When he demurred, her reply was blithe rather than bitter: 'Whatever I wear, I'll be criticized, so let's go for it.' Roland says: 'She liked to show her legs. She knew they were very good.'

And she knew she looked marvellous in her new working woman's uniform of sharply tailored little suits. Unless she was going to church, she wore them hatless but with vertiginous heels.

Those heels were a statement, too. Traditionally, stilettos are an assertion of sexual power but, for Diana, they also celebrated the fact that she had left behind a husband who was shorter than she was and for whose sake she had adopted flat shoes.

When Jimmy Choo became her favourite shoe designer in the early nineties, she would order shoes with virtually no heels but, as she grew more confident in herself, her heels grew higher.

'First she went to 2in, then 3in, then 3½in, then 3¾in. They just kept creeping up and up,' says Choo.

She never quite overcame the feeling, as she said, that people thought of her as 'the girl who likes shopping for clothes the whole time'.

That was certainly the case in some quarters. But by the summer of 1997, most people were looking beyond the clotheshorse and finding an altruistic, serious-minded and imaginative woman who didn't only wear clothes, but had learned to use them.

A lesser woman would have hidden herself away on the night her husband told the world that he had committed adultery, but not Diana. She blasted Charles off the front pages with this sexy, black, Christina Stambolian dress.

Surrounded by the stars of international fashion at a New York gala evening in 1995, Diana flies the flag in a sleek midnight blue silk sheath.

Arriving at the London Coliseum in July 1992 in an unusual bias cut, two-toned gown teamed with a clutch bag and shoes in the same fabric.

From the beginning, Diana understood that glamour was expected of her. Initially, she was guided by Anna Harvey of Vogue who introduced her to the cream of British fashion designers, but she quickly gained confidence and arrived at a clear view of what she wanted.

In the early years, she worked closely with the Emanuels, Bruce Oldfield and Victor Edelstein. But Catherine Walker, the shy French-born designer based in Chelsea, came to dominate the royal wardrobe – all the dresses featured here are by Diana's favourite evening wear designer.

When seventy-nine of the Princess's more formal gowns were auctioned for charity in New York in June 1997, the overwhelming majority were by Walker.

Edging towards a new elegance in a summery bare-shouldered floral gown for a film premiere in 1989.

A halter neck and cut-in armholes flaunt her strong shoulders and trim arms at the Albert Hall, 1995.

Diana laughed when she called this glamorous gown her Elvis dress; encrusted with rhinestones and decked with diamonds, she glittered as never before during an official visit to Hong Kong in 1989.

In a Catherine Walker pastel wool suit with fashionable bracelet-length sleeves for the Gold Awards at the Savoy, March 1997.

A crisp suit by Catherine Walker, inspired by nautical Chanel, at the Hilton, June 1995.

The perfect slip of a lavender dress by Versace in Sydney, November 1996.

By spring 1997, Diana was perfectly at ease in her dress-for-success working uniform: a trim, single-breasted Amanda Wakeley suit with a short pencil skirt.

Out for lunch in March 1997 in a Dior fringed Prince of Wales check trouser suit.

Confident and modern in a clean-lined Catherine Walker short sheath in July 1997.

After her divorce, Diana came into her own in terms of style. In her new role as a hard-working charity patron and campaigner, she was able to discount the limitations which her royal status had imposed on her dress sense.

To her pleasure, the skirts of her business suits got shorter as her heels got higher. She could also wear trouser suits, in which she felt comfortable, youthful and modern.

Another bonus was that she no longer felt constrained to wear clothes exclusively by British designers, a duty she had assumed without prompting before she married when it had become obvious that she would be perceived as a fashion ambassador. Although her working wardrobe included outfits from long-term favourites such as Tomasz Starzewski, the Princess also started to buy clothes by Dior, Chanel and Gianni Versace. The Italian designer was thrilled because it had been his dream to dress her ever since those first shy pictures of the newly engaged Lady Diana Spencer.

No longer shadowed by a lady-in-waiting to carry everything for her, the Princess abandoned tiny clutch bags for Chanel chain shoulder bags, chunky Hermès kelly bags, a Versace number decorated with gold Medusa head medallions, which the designer named after her, and her trusty Tanner Krolle briefcase.

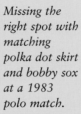

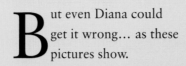

But even Diana could get it wrong... as these pictures show.

This ornate Rifat Ozbek jacket is just too glitzy, even for a 1987 rock concert.

Dungarees and a quilted bag: hippy look that's out of place at a 1981 polo match.

The Princess looks more dressed for bed than a 1985 London fashion show.

Missing the right spot with matching polka dot skirt and bobby sox at a 1983 polo match.

Matching coats at Easter 1987... never a good idea for mother or son.

Puffball can't work at Cannes, 1987.

Blending in with the railings at Spencer House, 1993.

A batty look in 1988 makes the Princess look like a frumpy Fifties district nurse.

Showing more than she intended at the London premiere of Oliver! in 1994.

Tracksuit pants tucked into cowboy boots are more at home on the range than the school run in April 1989.

Chapter 13

TOMORROW IS A MYSTERY

The astrological charts spread out on the coffee table indicated uproar and tremendous confusion. It was clear that if the Princess of Wales went ahead with her plan, she was going to face 'a long and painful journey'.

Diana listened closely. She had come to an arranged meeting with astrologer Felix Lyle at the Fulham home of their mutual friend, Dr James Colthurst.

She was so scared of the consequences of the step she intended to take that she needed to find out what the stars had to say about it. That step was going public about the misery and hypocrisy of her marriage to Prince Charles in Andrew Morton's controversial biography.

'Should I go ahead with it?' she asked Lyle. That was when he spread out his charts and explained how difficult it would be. She absorbed it all and shrugged. It would be hard, but the charts didn't say 'No'.

The fact that Diana consulted an astrologer before making the revelations that shook the throne had been a closely guarded secret.

'In the end, we agreed that she had a tremendous grievance,' says Lyle, speaking for the first time about their meeting. 'She was fighting for her independence and, despite my warning, she felt that this might be the only opportunity she would get to express how difficult it had been for her.'

So Diana went ahead, and Dr Colthurst became biographer Andrew Morton's faceless go-between and the courier of the tape recordings into which the Princess poured out her story night after night at her Kensington Palace home and which were to form the core of Morton's book.

From the early years of her marriage, Diana had consulted psychics, mystics and stargazers. The Princess

(Opposite): *Listening intently during a visit to the Royal Brompton Hospital in April 1997. In the whirlwind last few months of her life, Diana had a strange sense that she didn't have much time to achieve all that she wanted.*
(Above): *The Princess pictured at around the time of the publication of Andrew Morton's biography in 1992.*

Diana (circled) *runs towards the waiting helicopter after a 160-mile flying visit to introduce Dodi to her trusted psychic Rita Rogers.*

was no Nancy Reagan, who consulted the stars to guide her and her husband U.S. President Reagan's day-to-day movements, but Diana took astrology seriously enough to be mocked in royal circles for her dedication to so-called cranks.

She had a special interest in this area, for only after her death has it become apparent just how chillingly she had predicted her future.

Years before meeting Dodi Fayed, the man who shared her final weeks, she had talked about reaching a time when she could enjoy weekends in Paris, about the possibility of living abroad in France and of meeting someone 'who's foreign or has a lot of foreign blood in him'. Most poignantly, however, she said: 'I've got things to do and time is precious.'

Diana told Peter Settelen, who gave her lessons in public speaking: 'I do believe we know a bit about when we're going to go.' He felt that she sensed she didn't have much time to achieve all that she wanted.

While these insights, along with the advice she took from astrologers, psychics and clairvoyants, did not guide her day-to-day movements, the Princess had nurtured her spiritual side from childhood. She believed she was looked after 'in the spirit world' by her paternal grand-mother. Countess Spencer was one of the great beauties of her day who was courted by the then Prince of Wales (later the Duke of Windsor). He didn't marry her only

because, as the daughter of the Duke of Abercorn, she wasn't of royal blood.

Her married life to the 7th Earl Spencer was unhappy so the Countess, a sensitive and compassionate woman, threw herself into charitable works. Many believe Diana modelled herself on her grandmother.

Despite Diana's conviction that spiritual matters had their place in her life, she was fully aware that others did not share her beliefs. 'I'd never discuss it with anyone: they would think I was a nut,' she said.

Diana was among a growing number of people who consult mystic advisers about emotional matters or impor-tant decisions. So it was natural for her, when faced with the major step of deciding whether or not to help with the Morton biography, to have an astrological chart done.

It was her first meeting with Felix Lyle, who was one of several astrologers she consulted over the years.

In 1986 (the year Charles claimed he rekindled his affair with Camilla Parker Bowles in his television inter-view with Jonathan Dimbleby) Diana sought the advice of astrologer Penny Thornton, whom she had met through the Duchess of York. 'I just want to see if there's a light at the end of the tunnel,' she explained.

Between 1987 and 1992, Diana regularly consulted Betty Palko at her Surrey semi. Betty describes the Princess during those years as 'beautiful but sad. She had deep emotional problems and believed I could help.'

Leaving Dr Lily Hua Yu's acupuncture clinic in Camden Town, North London, in April 1997.

She repeatedly warned Diana she was being cheated on in her marriage and told her to beware of 'deceit and treachery'.

Later, Diana consulted Debbie Frank, who remained her astrologer until her death.

Less than three weeks before their deaths, the Princess and Dodi flew 160 miles by helicopter to see psychic Rita Rogers at her Derbyshire home. Speculation abounded as to what they discussed, but the significance of the visit was that Diana had introduced her new man to one of the most intimate and important areas of her life.

As well as the spiritual side of life, the Princess enjoyed New Age therapies including aromatherapy, homeopathy and acupuncture. She shared her beliefs, as well as studying books on the subject, with friends. She wrote to tell Richard Greene (whom she had met at the Chelsea Harbour Club) how much she had enjoyed reading the book *Journey Into Spiritual Healing* which he had given her.

Reincarnation was one subject Diana discussed with Richard over lunch. 'I'm not coming back,' she told him brightly, and he understood this to mean that she believed she would achieve everything she was meant to in her life.

She would sit cross-legged on the floor with Jimmy Choo, her shoe designer, and talk about his belief in Buddhism. Diana liked to meditate (though she found it difficult) and believed in the benefits of spiritual healing. For three years, healer Simone Simmons visited her once a week.

She had her Kensington Palace apartment rearranged by an expert in feng shui (the Chinese art of harmonious interior design) and she often wore a white crystal, symbolizing a clear mind, stability and harmony.

She liked the concept of t'ai chi (Chinese rhythmic exercise) yet she noticed how surprised people were when she gave her views about the energy flow it promotes.

'They look at me and say: "She's the girl who's supposed to like shopping for clothes the whole time. She's not supposed to know about spiritual things."'

Therapists came and went. Many of them felt that Diana's visits to them were more to do with her wish to engage with the world beyond the palace gates (for instance, she would insist on waiting her turn in their consulting rooms) rather than any great need for their treatments. But some, such as Ursula Gatley, to whom the Princess went twice a month for colonic irrigation, became trusted friends.

Others were dropped because she often suspected them of betraying confidences.

In the last year of her life, Diana had visited Dr Lily Hua Yu, a Chinese acupuncturist in Camden Town, North London. Six months after the Princess's death, Dr Lily went public with details of her treatment that dismayed Diana's family and friends.

Interestingly, the Princess said she stopped visiting the psychotherapist Susie Orbach in Swiss Cottage after two years because she found herself analyzing the therapist's problems rather than her own.

Diana spoke frequently about *deja vu* experiences and hearing voices. 'I've got a lot of that (*deja vu*). Places I think I've been before, people I've met,' she said.

It was this unusual gift that lay behind her decision to attend the 1988 party to mark the 40th birthday of Annabel Elliott, Camilla's sister, hosted by Lady Annabel Goldsmith at her home at Ham Common. The Princess said she had heard a voice compelling her to go.

That was the evening she startled other guests by asking them to leave her and Mrs Parker Bowles alone so she could confront her rival face-to-face about the affair she was having with the Prince of Wales. 'Boys, I'm just going to have a quick word with Camilla,' Diana announced.

The confrontation was on the ground floor, well away from the main party upstairs. The few people who were in the room retreated to a discreet distance but it was plain what was about to happen and one or two of them lingered.

The two women sat down and the Princess said: 'Camilla, I would just like you to know that I know exactly what is going on between you and Charles. I wasn't born yesterday.' But before Camilla could respond, the encounter was interrupted by someone who had been sent to end it.

It was not only as an adult that Diana claimed to have had premonitions. At thirteen, she had told her father, Earl Spencer: 'I'm going to marry someone who is in the public eye.' Four years later, while staying with friends in Norfolk, she had a vision that her father was going to be seriously ill.

Charles and his horse Allibar at Lambourn. Diana predicted the animal's sudden death in early 1981.

'I recalled saying: "I've got this strange feeling that he's going to drop down and, if he does, he'll die immediately, otherwise he'll survive." I heard myself say this and thought nothing more about it,' said Diana. 'Next day, the telephone rang and I said to my friends: "That will be about Daddy." It was – he'd collapsed.' The Earl survived but was crippled by the stroke he had suffered.

During her engagement in 1981, Diana had another premonition. While watching Charles, then a keen amateur jockey, put his mount, Allibar, through its paces at Lambourn, she suddenly said that the 11-year-old horse was going to have a heart attack and die. Within seconds, the animal reared and dropped to the ground, having suffered a coronary, and it did, indeed, die almost instantly.

Diana never claimed anything more than having 'instincts' about what was going to happen: 'I have feelings about things.' When Charles proposed to her, she heard a voice inside her say: 'You won't be Queen but you'll have a tough role.'

Despite her insights, the Princess was never one for mottoes or sayings, except for one that has a spiritual resonance: 'Today is the present, yesterday is history and tomorrow is a mystery.'

However, when she was feeling unloved in her marriage and her problems seemed beyond spiritual or professional help, it was her mother Frances Shand Kydd who usually dispensed comfort and advice.

They felt an additional kinship because the Princess knew that the Royal Family viewed her mother (as she was seen herself), as 'the baddie': the woman who had deserted her family for another man when Diana was six.

The Princess and her mother met quite often, usually in secret 'in many different places without anyone knowing,' says Frances. At other times, Diana would call her from wherever she was in the world 'at all times of the day and night'.

In 1988, when Frances's second husband, the businessman Peter Shand Kydd, left her after nineteen years of marriage, it was Diana's turn to offer a shoulder to cry on.

Before the Princess's separation from Charles in December 1992, her mother often stayed at Highgrove, the Waleses's country home. There could easily have been a difficult atmosphere between Frances and the Prince following an exchange between them at Harry's christening in 1984.

Charles had moaned to his mother-in-law that the Princess had given birth to another boy – and with 'rusty' (Spencer) hair to boot. Frances rounded on him, telling him that he should be grateful that his second son was healthy.

After that, she felt she had a new insight into her daughter's difficult life. Frances continued to visit Highgrove, but Charles was rarely there.

The Prince had no idea that when Diana made her will in June 1993 she had given her mother a special responsibility for watching over William and Harry's upbringing in the event of her own death. It would certainly have upset him because of the implication that he was incapable – without a Spencer input – of raising them successfully himself.

Frances was, of course, moved by Diana's decision and delighted. To her, this was her daughter's ultimate forgiveness for the disruption that her departure had caused in her children's lives. It comforts Frances to this day.

Chapter 14

INTO THE MINEFIELD

Sitting over coffee with her friend Susie Kassem in the cafeteria at London's Royal Brompton Hospital in February 1997, the Princess of Wales felt a touch at her elbow. A little girl of about seven stood there clutching a doctor's prescription. She wanted Diana's autograph. Behind her stood others, with pieces of paper, used envelopes, even parking tickets, and the Princess signed them all.

Mrs Kassem, a magistrate and wife of a leading financier, had first met Diana in September 1995 at the hospital bedside of a mutual friend, Joe Toffolo, the husband of Oonagh Toffolo, then Diana's acupuncturist, who was having a heart by-pass operation. Countless times since then she had witnessed the queues of people who gathered to meet the Princess and on each occasion she marvelled at her patience with them. This was the low-key Diana, in T-shirt and jeans, who would slip into hospital wards, often totally unex-

pected, and sit on patients' beds, stroking their hands.

The Diana who launched a crusade against land mines was another woman altogether. Her reaction to the terrible injuries caused by Man was very different from her response to sickness caused by nature.

In Angola in January last year, her mood was one of suppressed anger. You couldn't see it because of the magical effect she had on the victims she met. As Mrs Kassem says, it was 'like the sprinkling of fairy dust'. But inside, Diana was a cauldron. The scale of the unnecessary injuries reduced her to tears.

Yet back in London she found herself being drawn into a political slanging match which she simply couldn't understand. Earl Howe, then a junior defence minister, accused her of being a 'loose cannon' because her land-mines campaign was not entirely in line with Tory Government policy.

(Opposite): The Princess's magical ability to relate to suffering people during her Red Cross visit to Angola was more eloquent than any politician's speech about land mines.
(Above): Wreathed in smiles, Camilla arrives at Highgrove for her 50th birthday party, which was arranged by Prince Charles.

How could anyone, she asked, criticize what she was doing when all she wanted was to rid the world of mines?

The global scale of the attention on Diana's land-mines campaign surpassed anything she had ever done before, or anything she had imagined. She knew how to use her powers to win attention for the disadvantaged, but this was something new and she hated the controversy that raged over her.

It was all so very different from those schooldays at West Heath in Kent when, as a girl of sixteen who always had a mothering instinct, she volunteered to help people with learning difficulties at Darenth Park Hospital in nearby Dartford.

Muriel Stevens, who ran the hospital's volunteer service, taught the girls to 'lower yourselves to the patient's eye level, take their hands, look straight at them and talk to them'. How many pictures did we come to see of Diana doing just that?

'I would hate to take the credit for it,' says Mrs Stevens, now chief executive of the British Allergy Foundation. 'Diana was a natural. I remember her wonderful laugh. Everybody talks about her eyes, but her laugh was truly memorable.'

As well as going to the weekly dance at the hospital, Diana also became used to getting down on her hands and knees to crawl around with the patients.

It was to be eighteen years later in her Panorama interview that she was to use the phrase 'a Queen in people's hearts', five words she would come to regret. The mockery it attracted, fuelled by some of Prince Charles's supporters, wounded her deeply.

If she had not been at that time on the rise both mentally and physically – stronger, indeed, than she had been for years – she could easily have plummeted into despair again.

What helped her in coping with the critics at home was the warmth of the affection she was receiving abroad, especially in the United States. There she was embraced by everyone as a woman who simply wanted to make the world a better place.

Diana was desperate to be given a semi-official national role, completely non-political and involved solely with

Walking through a minefield literally as well as metaphorically: Diana in Angola in January 1997.

highlighting and helping the poor, sick and disadvantaged. It was the one talent she knew she had in abundance. Queen of Hearts exactly described what she had in mind.

John Major, the then Prime Minister, was a great supporter, but he was also mindful of Buckingham Palace's rather stiff attitude that if there was to be a non-political ambassadorial role it belonged to the Prince of Wales, not the Princess.

It was partly because her ambitions in this area had been thwarted that Diana gave the sensational Panorama

The sights she saw in Bosnia in August 1997 reduced Diana to tears of disbelief at man's inhumanity.

interview in November 1995 when she so memorably remarked that 'there were three of us in this marriage'. The belief has always been that her primary motive was revenge on her unfaithful husband but, in fact, she was equally concerned to let people know what she wanted to do with her life. Through television, she could go over the heads of her enemies at the Palace.

In official circles, it had the opposite effect to the one she had intended. It quite wrongly marked her down as unreliable and unstable. She was nothing of the kind, but it took the land mines campaign to prove how foolish – and in some cases wicked – her critics had been.

It was Lord 'Dickie' Attenborough who introduced the Princess to the cause when he invited her to a film premiere in aid of the Red Cross, which was seeking a world ban on mines. For some years, Diana had been involved in breaking down the prejudices surrounding Aids and had become a well-known face in cancer wards. She could comfort but do little else for these sufferers.

With land mines, she realized it was within her power to make a difference. The few days she spent in Angola with the Red Cross captured the world's imagination. And it transformed Diana: she felt she could really achieve something.

She didn't stop there. In Washington, her impassioned speech about the horror of mines so impressed Hillary Clinton that the President's wife invited her to the White House to discuss it, a bold gesture because the U.S. still made and used land mines.

In Britain, the new Labour Government shrewdly saw the value in harnessing the Princess's universal popularity, and Tony Blair invited her to lunch at Chequers, his official country home. Diana took Prince William, for she believed it was important for her son, as next in line to the throne after Charles, to meet the Prime Minister.

It was an exciting occasion because Blair confided that he and Bill Clinton had discussed what kind of role she might have. Later, she told Gulu Lalvani all about it.

'Blair and Diana didn't come to any conclusions during that lunch but agreed to meet again to come up with something more concrete,' says Lalvani.

'I asked her what she would say if Blair asked what she wanted to do. She said she felt she could act as a mediator between fighting countries. She told me: "I know I can be a peacemaker because people trust me."

Diana's impassioned speech on land mines in Washington in June 1997 echoed round the world.

South-West London. She was in the Royal Marsden being treated for cancer in 1994 when the door of the ward opened and, to everyone's surprise, in walked the Princess.

Diana chatted with the patients one by one, sitting on their beds. A neighbour who was visiting Mrs Taylor when Diana arrived couldn't stop herself from saying: 'You're very tall, aren't you?' Mrs Taylor recalls: 'The Princess drew herself up as tall as possible, laughing, and replied: "Well, you should see me in my high heels." '

Just before she went to Bosnia last August on her last land mines mission, the Princess could be seen driving from her Kensington Palace home with the back seat of her blue BMW filled with sweets, balloons, videos and gift-wrapped toys from Hamley's. Despite the frenzy of those last whirlwind weeks, she was on her way once again to see sick children in a London hospital.

After so many years, such an excursion might have become routine, but for Diana it never was. It was always 'an adventure'. It was the same when she invited some of the patients and their families to her home. 'Let's give them a day to remember,' she would tell her butler Paul Burrell. One time, he was dispatched to buy a Batman outfit for a boy suffering from leukaemia.

Diana loved giving because, as she once said: 'There are no strings.' Equally, she would say: 'I am not a good receiver.' She was never happier than when she was making someone else happy. As her friend Susie Kassem puts it: 'I can only say that, like doctors, nurses or priests, she had a calling. It's all the more remarkable that she fulfilled it despite the circumstances of her private life.'

By the summer of 1997, Diana finally felt she was being recognized by the world as a woman who could really make a difference in people's lives. But the memories of her unhappy marriage still had the power to cast a shadow over her life. As she set out on the holiday in the South of France during which she would find love, she discovered that Prince Charles was hosting a 50th birthday party for Camilla Parker Bowles at Highgrove on Friday, 18 July, the very day the Princess had intended to return to Britain. The thought of it so tormented her that she couldn't bring herself to come home until the Sunday when it was all over and done with.

She knew if she were involved with something then people would take notice.'

Diana had allowed a BBC documentary film crew to accompany her to Angola because she recognized the power of television in exposing world problems.

She was also planning a television programme on social issues in South Africa with her brother Charles, a television journalist, and another, with Lalvani's help, on the Aids epidemic in Bombay. But while this work gave her immense satisfaction, she would never have given up her hospital visits and the laughter that rang out in the wards as she moved from patient to patient.

She had been making private, informal visits for years to the leading London hospitals. Often, she would phone in advance to say she was coming, but sometimes she arrived unannounced.

Typical of what went on when Diana visited a hospital is remembered by 59-year-old Iris Taylor, of Southfields,

Chapter 15

A NEW LOVE

When, in September 1996, Mohamed Al Fayed asked the newly divorced Princess of Wales if she would like to be a director of Harrods, she took it as a light-hearted suggestion and declined.

Al Fayed was naturally disappointed. Diana on the board of the international division of his flagship store would have been the envy of every other boardroom in the world. The Princess's stepmother Raine, Countess Spencer, had recently become a non-executive director of Harrods International, but Diana explained politely that, under the terms of her divorce, she was not allowed to involve herself in any commercial enterprise.

However, the businessman had not exhausted his deepest hopes as far as the Princess was concerned. He was anxious that she should meet his son Dodi because, he told her, he was sure they would get on.

He dreamed of such a match and had been heard urging Dodi in that direction. Only Al Fayed, with his life of indulgence, could have been at the centre of such a theatrical alliance.

Ten months later, in July 1997, a helicopter painted in the cream, gold and green Harrods livery landed on the grass at Kensington Palace and Diana climbed aboard with an excited William and Harry. Within half an hour, they were setting down at Stansted airport in Essex and transferring to a waiting Gulfstream executive jet from Al Fayed's aviation charter company's fleet. It was the start of one of the most dramatic and tragic episodes in British public life.

The jet took the royal party to Nice airport where a limousine waiting on the tarmac whisked them to the harbour. Then it was a boat ride across the bay to St Tropez. Finally they arrived at Al Fayed's £10 million home in the sun, an eight-acre compound with every conceivable delight. There, also, was the handsome 42-year-old man Al Fayed was longing for Diana to get to know: his son Dodi.

Dodi's girlfriend, the former Calvin Klein model Kelly Fisher, was also there, although staying on a boat in the harbour and not as a guest in the Al Fayed compound. After a few days, Dodi and his girlfriend left. A day or so later, he returned alone.

(Opposite): *Princess Diana alone with her thoughts on the diving board of Al Fayed's 195ft yacht Jonikal off Portofino, Italy, on 24 August.*
(Above): *Diana with Dodi, the man who captivated her.*

Diana and Dodi were not strangers. They had met ten years earlier at Smith's Lawn, Windsor, when Dodi and Prince Charles were in opposing polo teams. There had been other casual meetings at film premieres where Dodi, a Hollywood producer whose films included the Oscar-winning *Chariots Of Fire*, was a familiar figure. But they had never got to know each other.

Now, within the intimate family compound which Al Fayed and his Finnish-born wife Heini loved so much, Diana and Dodi were pointedly left to talk.

They found they had much in common. Indeed, Diana was struck by the fact that their lives had followed parallel courses and had brought each of them to a point where they were looking for similar futures.

Like the Princess, Dodi's parents had parted when he was small. As with Diana, custody was given to his father and he missed his mother Samira Khashoggi, sister of the arms dealer Adnan Khashoggi. Mother and son retained a good relationship until her death eleven years ago.

Like Diana, Dodi had made an unhappy marriage, although his ended quickly and there were no children. Where Diana developed a compulsive eating disorder, bulimia, Dodi had discovered another compulsion: cocaine.

Like Diana, who yearned for a daughter, Dodi wanted children – and soon. She found Dodi the man to be very different from his reputation as a playboy. He told her he wanted to settle down.

So here was a man with, as the Princess put it, 'all the toys', whose company she and her sons delighted in, and whose family could provide the privacy that she craved. Dodi had one additional, crucial attribute, unusual in a man in his forties with everything to offer: he was single. Diana and Dodi found that, quite apart from his father's ambitions for them, they really did like each other.

As the days went by aboard Al Fayed's yacht, the Jonikal, and in the compound, their feelings for each other began to develop into something considerably deeper.

Al Fayed felt a special empathy for the Princess. Like himself, he saw her as a victim of the British Establishment, forced to live as an outsider. He was making himself into something of a father figure to the Princess. Diana's own beloved father had died in 1992.

She adored the protective way Al Fayed and his family looked after her and the boys. All this and romance as well.

Suddenly, Diana's world, troubled for so many years, was filled with the heady anticipation of a totally unexpected future. She and Dodi were in love. Just how totally – or what ultimately it might have led to – is impossible to gauge. But Diana's closest friend and mother figure, Lucia Flecha de Lima, wife of Brazil's former ambassador in London and now in Washington, believes she was captivated by the affection of 'a man who had no full-time occupation and could dedicate all his time to her, something she had never had in her life'.

And yet Diana's new world was still far from perfect. The holiday with Dodi and the Al Fayed family had helped erase from her mind 'the grief of my past', but not entirely.

She had taken to St Tropez the troubled thoughts of an ex-wife and mother who had just been told via a Channel 5 television documentary on Camilla Parker Bowles that Charles had 'never loved' his wife. This claim

That last summer holiday together in St Tropez was full of hugs for Prince Harry (left) *and adventure for Prince William* (opposite). *Diana was delighted that her sons seemed so happy in the company of her new friends.*

hurt Diana deeply because she knew it to be untrue and because of the effect she feared it could have on William and Harry.

'He did love me and I loved him,' she told her close friend and astrologer Debbie Frank in a telephone call.

Nevertheless, she did her best not to allow the allegation to overshadow her happiness. Just five days after returning to Britain with her sons, Diana and Dodi slipped away together for a weekend in Paris.

He took her to the Duke and Duchess of Windsor's former home in the Bois de Boulogne, which his father has owned since 1987. Had they married, Diana and Dodi may well have lived there.

The Princess's friends were aware that something special was happening in her life. 'I've met someone,' was how she put it to Debbie Frank and other close friends. None of them had heard her use that expression before and they saw it as highly significant.

At the beginning of August, Diana and Dodi went back to the Mediterranean for five blissful days alone on board the Jonikal. It was then that pictures of them embracing were published round the world.

For once, Diana's hatred of the *paparazzi* was temporarily transcended by a deeper emotion. She believed the love affair had a future and she was unconcerned that the world knew about it.

In Dodi, she was certain she had found someone who loved her for what she was and with whom she could just be herself. For the first time in many years, she felt safe.

August was a frenzied month for Diana. Nothing, not even her need to be with Dodi, was going to stop her making her anti-personnel mines visit to Bosnia or spending a pre-arranged holiday with her friend Rosa Monckton, the wife of *Sunday Telegraph* editor Dominic Lawson.

Rosa had, in fact, strongly advised Diana not to holiday with the controversial Mohamed Al Fayed whose unsavoury 'brown envelope' dealings with Tory MPs had been receiving a great deal of publicity, but she found her friend bubbling with happiness after finding romance. 'She liked the feeling of having someone who not only so obviously cared for her but was not afraid to be seen doing so,' said Rosa.

Dodi was very different from the other men who had figured in Diana's life after her marriage had foundered.

Each of the others, in their own way, had felt as great a need for secrecy as she had. She had feared for them, knowing that exposure could change their lives.

'Who would take me on?' she had lamented. 'I have so much baggage. Anyone who takes me out has to accept the fact that their business will be raked over in the papers. I think I am safer alone.'

What was so refreshing about Dodi was that he was prepared to live his own life and didn't care what others made of it. The one exception was his father, of whom he was scared and who could be scathing with him, but there would hardly be criticism from that quarter with the Princess on his arm.

The Princess's exuberant leap into a motor launch says so much about her state of mind.

When Diana came back from her five-day trip with Rosa to the Greek islands, Dodi was waiting for her. They were reunited at his Park Lane penthouse. The following day, they left for the French Riviera and sailed to Sardinia. From there, nine days later, they flew to Paris.

It was 30 August and Dodi went to the chic Repossi jewellers on the Place Vendôme, close to the Ritz Hotel owned by his father, to collect a ring he had bought Diana.

She let him buy it without the protests that had preceded the delivery of other expensive gifts. His extravagance was the one area in their relationship about which she felt decidedly uneasy. 'I don't want to be bought,' she protested to friends.

She got angry when he would phone and, as Rosa Monckton says, 'recite a list of the presents he had bought her'. It was not what she wanted but Diana reluctantly had to accept that this compulsive giving was Dodi's way of showing her how much he loved her.

That evening, they had dinner at the Ritz. Then they were driven off at speed towards his apartment. The journey was never completed...

Chapter 16

DIANA'S LEGACY

This was not the destiny Diana had imagined as a child. Her death was a kind of martyrdom, sainthood almost, with people throwing flowers at her coffin and policemen on crowd control dragging gloved hands hastily across moistening eyes.

A congregation's applause rose to the vaulted rafters of Westminster Abbey for the first time in its 750-year history, and a monarch had bent the knee to the will of an angry people and broken tradition to fly the Union Flag at half-mast at Buckingham Palace for a woman who was no longer an HRH.

Diana had never wanted this. All that she had sought in her thirty-six years was to be loved for herself and to be allowed to use her gifts to bring comfort to other people, a simple enough wish list for anyone, let alone a Princess.

Everything that was always so tantalizingly just out of her reach in the Princess of Wales's life came together as the country united in mass mourning.

Even Prince Charles, whom she had never ceased to love and who had certainly loved her once, effectively

came back to her as he accepted condolences from solemn crowds with outstretched hands. It felt almost as though he and Diana had never divorced.

Every bloom thrown by a caring hand in front of the hearse bearing her away from the people to the island resting place at Althorp, her family's ancestral home, was more than an expression of love and affection. Each was also a condemnation of the stiff, unseen Establishment that had averted its eyes when Diana's needs were at their most critical.

The sense of loss that swept over the nation was at the same time a warm surge of togetherness. In the week between Diana's death and her funeral, young mothers with pushchairs and leather-jacketed bikers added their bunches of flowers to the lakes of summer blooms outside the gates of her home, Kensington Palace.

People from all walks of life were prepared to queue for up to twelve hours to sign the books of condolence all over the country. There was electricity in the air, a sense of purpose.

(Above): *Of all the floral tributes, the most poignant was this simple bouquet and its handwritten card from Princes William and Harry.* (Opposite): *Diana visitig a mosque in Egypt in May 1992.*

There was also at first during that extraordinary week a feeling of censure towards the Prince of Wales, an instinctive judgment that he had let down Diana.

He felt it himself, rising at dawn to walk the Balmoral moorland for an hour, accompanied only by his thoughts.

The Prince was filled with remorse when, a few hours after doctors at the Pitié-Salpetrière hospital in Paris had pronounced Diana dead from the injuries she received when the car carrying her and Dodi smashed into a pillar in an underpass, he flew to France with her sisters Sarah and Jane to bring home her body.

Almost exactly a year earlier, when the end of their fifteen-year marriage had been made absolute, Diana had been stripped of the title HRH, Her Royal Highness. Now the Prince, plainly distressed at his ex-wife's death, was most concerned that she should receive all the honour and trappings befitting a full member of the Royal Family.

He personally made sure that after arriving back at RAF Northolt, her coffin was escorted by the requisite royal allocation of seven police motorcycle outriders on its journey into London.

Then he flew back to join the Royal Family at Balmoral, where his sons William and Harry, their faces bleached by shock, had, to many people's surprise, been taken on a public drive to church that Sunday morning, with the Queen saying that they must maintain 'business as usual'.

Stoicism and tradition have their place, but there was an unease and dismay at what was happening at Balmoral. In fact, many felt that *nothing* seemed to be happening.

Elsewhere in Britain, the national mood of sadness was marked by open bewilderment that the only public building in Britain not flying a flag at half-mast was Buckingham Palace.

The Royal Family was still in Balmoral and, apart from a brief statement, had remained silent on Diana's death.

The Royals were aware, however, of the growing criticism that they were cold and uncaring, charges that were levelled at them not only by the media but also by the crowds outside Buckingham Palace. Mourners pointed at the empty flagpole and put their anger in one word: Why?

(Left): *Princess Diana's grieving mother, Frances Shand Kydd, leaving Westminster Abbey.*

(Opposite): *Tears for a Princess at the funeral* (left to right): *A policewoman on duty can't hide her feelings; families try to comfort each other; the Duchess of York has to struggle to retain her composure.*

(Below): *At RAF Northolt, the Princess's coffin receives full military honours on its arrival home in Britain from Paris.*

The official reason was protocol. The flagpole flew the sovereign's Standard, and only when she was in residence. It was explained that the Royals had not left Balmoral because they wanted to surround William and Harry in a protective tranquillity impossible to attain in London.

But some of Diana's friends found these explanations unconvincing. To them, this was the Royal Family behaving towards Diana pretty much as it always had.

The pressure was building up in the streets. What had started off as puzzlement became open anger.

There was concern at Scotland Yard and among senior Palace courtiers that the Princess's funeral presented a possibility of demonstrations against the Royal Family, especially Prince Charles.

But then, just as quickly, the mood changed and softened. First, the route was doubled in length to enable twice as many people to say goodbye to the young woman Tony Blair described so accurately as the 'People's Princess'.

Then it was announced that a flag *would* be flown at half-mast at Buckingham Palace, though on a different flagpole. And then the inexplicable silence was broken. The Royal Family returned to London from Scotland a day earlier than planned, emerging from their isolation to accept condolences from the public and to look at all the flowers.

On the eve of the funeral, the Queen broadcast live to the nation from Buckingham Palace. Her words clearly, as she said, came from the heart.

She spoke 'as a grandmother' about 'an exceptional and gifted human being' whom she 'admired and respected' and who 'in good times and bad… never lost her capacity to smile and laugh, nor to inspire others with her warmth and kindness… No one who knew Diana will ever forget her'.

At last, the grieving millions had heard what they wanted to hear. The rift was over. The Royal Family was back in the bosom of the nation.

Against all the odds and mindful of her troubled marriage and life, the Princess of Wales's funeral had become a defining moment of reconciliation between the monarchy and its people.

A policeman adds a bouquet to the ocean of flowers outside Kensington Palace.

Had Diana been able to script her own finale, this rapprochement would have been it. For despite the stress and embarrassment that exposure of her palace life had laid at the Royal Family's door, Diana never stopped believing passionately in the monarchy. She wanted her son William to be King and to be loved by his people.

Indeed, everything we have seen of the Royal Family's new image since suggests that, far from damaging the monarchy, Diana has laid down a blueprint for change which is likely to be its salvation.

Her death, and the events that followed, convinced the Royals that Diana's way of communicating with the people was the way the nation wanted it to be, less formal and more intimate, a closeness that those born into the Royal Family had never achieved.

People realized that they had rarely seen the Queen without her gloves and that she had accepted posies from a thousand curtsying little girls but had never seemed to have reached out and touched a child.

Other Royals were no different. The Princess Royal had even admitted on television that she didn't much like children and she certainly had never been known, in all her global travels for Save the Children, to cuddle a youngster.

Comparisons between the other Royals' approach and the easy way Diana would hug the victims of nature's cruellest afflictions had been made, of course, during the Princess's life. The inevitable comparison disconcerted the Royals and yet they had found it impossible to change their ways.

One royal aide who saw their discomfort at close hand believes the Royals stuck to their dated, distant ways because to do anything else would invite comparison with the way Diana did it. Only once she had gone did they feel able to attempt the closeness with ordinary people which had come so naturally to the Princess.

Indeed, it may be argued that, since Diana's death, the other Royals have tried their best to be like her. Who would ever have imagined the Queen holding out her hand for a session of reflexology in front of the cameras, as she did in December 1997?

(Right and overleaf): *Side by side outside St James's Palace, the Duke of Edinburgh, William, Earl Spencer, Harry and Prince Charles silently watch the arrival of the Princess's coffin.*

142

When someone in the crowd handed the Queen a balloon after she and Prince Philip emerged from their golden wedding thanksgiving service at Westminster Abbey in November 1997, she resisted the impulse to pass it to a lady-in-waiting as she has done at other such moments all her life and held on to it instead as she continued her walkabout.

Meanwhile, Prince Charles has gone out of his way to demonstrate his credentials as a loving – but, crucially, modern – father. Taking Prince Harry on an official visit to South Africa last November was a breakthrough. The last time something comparable had occurred was early in his marriage when he and Diana took 9-month-old William to Australia and New Zealand.

(Below): *Eight young pallbearers of the 1st Battalion Welsh Guards bear the Princess's coffin into Westminster Abbey.*

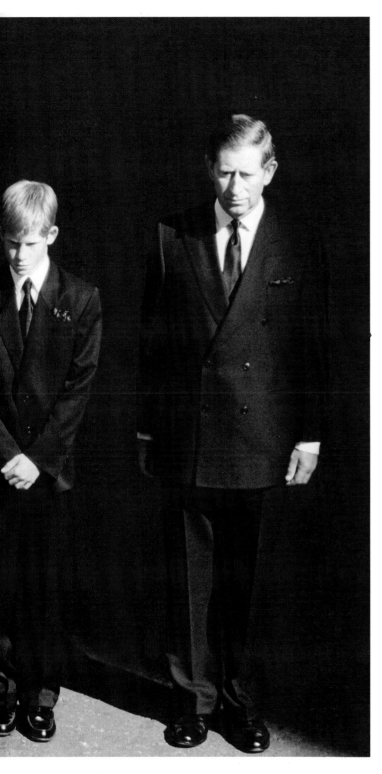

And what a different Prince of Wales we saw, joking for the cameras, jesting with reporters, a warm-hearted father who was quite unrecognizable from the solemn cardboard cut-out that he used to be.

Lucia Flecha de Lima, the wife of the former Brazilian ambassador in London, recalls Charles as 'timid, formal and exclusively oriented for preparation to become King'.

When Diana was alive, Charles considered his sons' upbringing to be 'private territory' and – with the exception of the Queen Mother's birthday – there were only glimpses of the young Princes' progress. But in recent months, he has shared his sons with the people.

The Royals had always recognized Diana's empathy with ordinary people but it was not until her death and the

*Many threw flowers on to the bonnet of the hearse as it made its way
through the streets of North London filled with silent mourners.*

amazing public demonstration of affection for her that they grasped what lay behind her universal popularity.

No wonder that on her golden wedding day less than three months after Diana's tragic death, the Queen spoke so revealingly about the importance of public opinion to the continued existence of the Royal Family.

She said that being a Royal meant that 'the message is often harder to read, obscured as it can be by deference, rhetoric or the conflicting currents of public opinion. But read it we must'. No one had ever heard any senior Royal complain publicly about deference before. Certainly, the Queen had never been known to speak so candidly.

Now, in the anxious atmosphere of post-Diana change, the Union Flag flies from Buckingham Palace even when the Queen is not there. There is talk of cutting down on the number of palaces and even reducing the number of Royals involved in ceremonial duties.

The 'Way Ahead' group led by the Queen has suggested pruning most of the twenty-two Royals bearing the style HRH (which was taken from Diana), restricting the remaining Royal Highnesses to the monarch and those closest to her or him, barely a handful. In another modernizing surge, they have indicated that bowing and curtsying should in future be 'optional'.

Diana's legacy is that everyone has gained from her sixteen years as a Princess. She focused attention on areas of hopelessness here and around the world that previously had to struggle for attention.

The monarchy appears prepared to modernize itself, to be accountable and less distant, freed from the strait-jacket of outmoded formality.

Diana left behind a Royal Family that is, paradoxically, more secure, not less so, because of her revolutionary style.

But as the lawyer Lord Mishcon, her friend and confidant who oversaw the divorce settlement, muses: 'If only things could have been different... what a wonderful Queen we could have had.'

*Two days after the funeral, Earl Spencer walks through the
carpet of flowers covering his sister's island resting place.*

Chapter 17

THE WAY AHEAD

Only the most fanciful of prophets would have predicted that the little girl who dreamed of marrying for love would come to exert such influence on the world that it would continue irresistibly after her death, and even be accelerated by it.

Global views on fashion, disease, poverty and even warfare... Princess Diana touched them all. There was only one place where you would never have expected to find her thinking supplanting what was already in place: the monarchy.

Yet since the Paris car crash which killed her on 31 August 1997 elements of the Princess's style have been tangibly present at hundreds of official engagements, home and abroad, carried out by the Royal Family.

All of the Royals have been affected, to differing degrees. Even Princess Anne, that most arch of royal figures, appears to have unbent a little.

The Prince of Wales has been doing his best to encompass the friendly approach which made his late ex-wife such a favourite with the people.

But what has been happening in those other, less public areas? How have her sons really been coping with their loss?

During the relatively brief period since their mother's death, both of the boys have changed, but in significantly different ways.

There is something different about 16-year-old Prince William now, an air of self-reliance that sprang up almost from the moment of his mother's death. It was first noticed in the quiet manner of his grief, the maturity with which he bore the pain.

How uncannily like Diana he is. Her bearing, her golden hair. Tall and athletic just like her. Even his smile is hers, and that gentleness with which, merely days after he had lost his beloved mother, he was able to receive flowers from the crowds and, astonishingly, smile and say: 'Thank you so much.'

There is, indeed, much about him that is Diana. And yet in the bleak months since her death, a different William has emerged.

(Opposite): A charming 1994 portrait of Diana, 12-year-old William and 10-year-old Harry by John Swannell.(Above): Prince William and Prince Harry on their first skiing trip since the death of their mother in Klosters in January 1998.

(Opposite): *Thirteen-year-old William's admiring glance at Prince Charles, who is wearing his medals for the 50th anniversary of VJ Day in August 1995, reveals everything about their relationship.*

(Right): *Prince Charles is obviously enjoying this boisterous toboggan ride with 12-year-old Harry during their ski trip to Klosters in January 1997.*

He has revealed himself as what his mother always knew him to be, not so much a volatile Spencer as a disciplined member of the House of Windsor.

Unexpectedly perhaps for a boy associated so closely with his mother, William is in reality much more like his father: controlled, studied in his manner and never likely to let his feelings show either in public or in private.

There are, it must be said, crucial differences: he is not weak and he doesn't blame others, either for his own shortcomings or the misfortunes of life.

Since Diana's death, William has been 13-year-old Harry's comforter and counsel, looking after his younger brother with a fondness and a protective arm that would have delighted his mother, who knew what it was like to need help.

For his part, Harry has leaned heavily on his big brother, knowing instinctively that he can rely on him.

Harry is a 'young thirteen'. At that age, William's voice had broken, but Harry's hasn't. Until his mother's death, he was the happy-go-lucky one who often teased his big brother about the responsibilities he faced as King.

He still is like this at times, but the family has noticed that he no longer has quite the same relentless appetite for fun. He spends a lot of his time deep in thought.

Had Princess Diana lived, Harry is unlikely to have gone to Eton College like his brother, but to a less academically pressured school such as Radley or Milton Abbey, both of which are anxious to take him. But now, more than ever, Prince Charles wants Harry to join William at Eton this September because he, too, understands how

With his shy smile and his inclined head, 15-year-old William looks uncannily like his mother, pictured here during a holiday at Balmoral in August 1997. Two weeks later, Diana was dead.

much the younger boy needs his brother. And Charles is aware that William is just the 'man' for the job.

When the two Princes made their final visit to their mother's home in Kensington Palace in February to choose mementoes, William, typically, coaxed Harry through the apartment where they shared so many happy times with Diana.

Both boys selected some photographs of the Princess in silver frames and some of the twenty or so stuffed animals that had been her companions since childhood, when she would take them to bed for comfort.

All of the boys' possessions had already been transferred to their new London home, York House in St James's Palace, where Prince Charles instructed interior designer Robert Kime to recreate the boys' old bedrooms as closely as possible.

Even the carpets were lifted from Kensington Palace and relaid. They also took one practical item that had been forgotten in the move. This was the pub-sized television installed for them by Diana just a few weeks before her death and on which they like to watch films, videos and sport.

Life for the two young Princes is very different from how it was before their mother's death.

Until the tragedy, they divided their holidays between their mother in London and their father at Highgrove or one of the other royal palaces.

While they adored being with their mother, Diana knew, regretfully, that they didn't much like London. William especially (how like his father) much prefers the country and its pursuits.

Princess Diana, without a country home of her own, could offer them only an unchanging metropolitan diet. But now with their father they can have the choice of both town and country.

Charles is also learning to give his boys both sides of himself. While his ex-wife was alive, he was never, despite stories to the contrary that have been emanating from his circle, the kind of father who romped with his sons. But he does now.

Diana and 9-year-old Harry arrive at church at Sandringham bearing gifts on Christmas Day 1993. Less than an hour after the service, the Princess kissed her sons goodbye and drove away to spend the rest of the festivities without her family.

Delightful highlights of William and Harry's contented childhoods.

Despite his mother's helping hand, the 13-year-old William signed the wrong page of the register on his first day at Eton in September 1995. Although the Waleses had been separated for nearly three years, Diana was always keen to give her sons as normal a family life as possible.

For the first time since those early years of marriage when Diana tried in vain to persuade him to spend time with the infant Princes in the nursery, Charles makes a point of being with his two sons as much as possible, particularly in trying to keep his official diary as empty as possible during the 140 days a year that they are home from school.

The old Prince Charles at times seemed a slightly distant father, which was probably a legacy of his own upbringing which lacked physical comforting from either of his parents and left him feeling rather unloved.

It always hurt Diana that, after their separation, he needed a woman to help him look after the boys.

Her resentment at the way 'surrogate mother' Tiggy Legge-Bourke, Charles's one-time personal assistant, rather overwhelmed the young Princes with affection became a major issue in the final years of their marriage.

Tiggy, with all her Sloaney exuberance, remains a central figure in the young Princes' lives – she is hugely popular with Harry. Even the Princess's most loyal friends now recognise that Charles needs her help because of the kind of man he is.

But Tiggy is not infallible. It was her decision to take the Princes to see the Beaufort Hunt riding out in the winter on one of the very days that Camilla Parker Bowles, Charles's long-time mistress, was among the riders.

Pictures of the Princes taken by local photographers caused a major controversy. Although they were not published, Charles was furious. Tiggy was reprimanded for being careless.

Now thirty-three and unmarried, Tiggy remains ever available to help out whenever she is summoned.

And at the heart of all decisions in Charles's household is the crucial question of what is best primarily for William, but also, of course, for Harry.

Everyone, from police bodyguards to lowly aides, believes they have the answer. Ironically, those who spend most time with William find themselves believing that he is rapidly becoming a young man who will find the answer for himself.

In Diana's will, which was published in March 1997, it was stated that she wished her mother Frances Shand Kydd and her brother Earl Spencer to have a hand in her sons' upbringing.

The reality of this request is that although the two Princes do see their mother's family, contact is limited. William has talked with his uncle and been out shooting with him, and the Princess's sisters Jane and Sarah have done their best to fulfil what they know was Diana's unspoken wish for them to stay in close touch with her boys.

Lady Jane Fellowes, who is married to the Queen's Private Secretary Sir Robert Fellowes, regularly stands on the touchline at Ludgrove, Harry's present school, to watch him play football.

Harry has also been to stay with his other aunt, Lady Sarah McCorquodale, who has three children and lives in Lincolnshire with her farmer husband Neil.

And yet there is a feeling among friends of the Spencers that the family's contact with the two young Princes can never live up to the pledge to let their souls 'sing openly' made by Earl Spencer in his impassioned oration at Diana's Westminster Abbey funeral.

'The family would never force themselves on the boys – they just want them to know that they are there,' says a Spencer friend. 'What they are finding, however, is that although they can reach the boys during term time, it seems harder to make contact with them during the school holidays.'

Prince Charles's friends, it must be said, thought Earl Spencer was being 'rather presumptuous' to talk so loftily of Diana's family helping to bring up the Princes. Royal circles know that Spencer's brotherly pledge irritated the Prince of Wales, who regards as 'impertinent' any suggestion that he does not know how to bring up his own children.

And where does Camilla Parker Bowles, Prince Charles's long-time mistress, come into all this? The answer is that she is neither a family topic nor an issue.

The practice of her not being around when the two young Princes are with their father, and vice versa, continues. She never stays overnight at Highgrove, the

The ever helpful Tiggy carries the bags in February 1994 as the three Princes arrive at Zurich airport at the start of their annual ski holiday in Klosters.

Prince's country estate, or St James's Palace, his London base, when the boys are home from school.

Meanwhile, the two young Princes have been drawn to the bosom of the Royal Family much more tightly than before. They see more of the Queen than at any time in their lives. William continues to take tea with his grandmother at Windsor Castle just across the Thames from Eton College on Sunday afternoons, and Harry will join them after, as hoped, he goes to Eton in September.

The other week, the Queen made an unprecedented visit to the ancient college, taking her seat among

Two days after Charles and Diana's divorce in August 1996, photographers were tipped off that Camilla would be meeting her daughter Laura, then eighteen, at Chippenham station. The campaign to slowly introduce the Prince's mistress to the public abruptly ended when Diana died. She remains an invisible presence in William and Harry's lives.

How the two young Princes have changed: From stiffly formal little boys (above, in June 1989 at Beating the Retreat at Kensington Palace) to smiling, relaxed teenagers (opposite, arriving with Prince Charles at December's premiere of the film Spiceworld).

parents and friends to see Prince William in Shakespeare's *The Tempest*, in which he had the small part of an attendant lord. But it is largely Prince Philip's influence which has grown since the death of Diana. Philip, who is the real boss of the House of Windsor, was often brusque with Diana, but he has always had a fond relationship with his grandson William. Perhaps he recognizes in him strengths which, to his regret, the Prince of Wales does not have.

Since Diana's death he has become closer than ever to William. The boy and his grandfather talk a lot about life and family matters, as well as the future.

These conversations often take place when, with guns under their arms, they go duck shooting, usually

with William's favourite cousin Peter Phillips, Princess Anne's son.

The untitled 20-year-old rugby-playing Peter has assumed the mantle of 'big brother' to both William and Harry. His 16-year-old sister Zara, who went skiing with the Princes and their father in Klosters in the Swiss Alps in January, is also a favourite with them.

And what about the Princes' relationship with Princesses Beatrice, aged nine, and 8-year-old Eugenie? When their mother, the Duchess of York, was Diana's best friend, the children were an inseparable foursome.

In the summer, the boys could escape the confines of Diana's Kensington Palace apartment and swim in Fergie's pool at Romenda Lodge near Windsor as their mothers discussed the problems of single parenthood. They all went on holidays together to the South of France and they often skied together.

Sadly, the little girls see almost nothing of their cousins these days and miss them a lot. While their fathers Charles and Andrew get on well enough as brothers, the problem is Fergie's excesses for which the Royal Family in general, and the Prince of Wales in particular, feel a profound distaste.

Though she had fallen out with Diana, Fergie has told friends that she believes that sooner or later there would have been a reconciliation and all would have been well again.

When Diana died, there was so much in her life that was poised to be well again. Most of all, she knew that William and Harry were growing up, moving towards the moment in their lives when all the unpleasantness and divisions that scarred their childhood would ease.

Clearly, they are not yet out of the woods. It takes time. But Diana's influence on them is there to see. How proud she would have been.

Diana, 9-year-old William and 7-year-old Harry on a visit to Niagara Falls in October 1991.

INDEX

(Numbers in *italics* refer to illustrations)

Russell, Adam, 30

S

Sadat, President Anwar and Mme Jihan, 52

St James's Palace, *142–3*; York House, 153

St Paul's Cathedral, 46–8

St Tropez, Diana in, 70, *71*, 105, *105*, 131–2, *132–3*, 134

Sandringham, 58, 64, 75, 81, *153*; *see also* Park House

Sarah, Duchess of York (Fergie), 45, 46, 68, 86, 87, 100, 103, 120, *139*, 160

Savoy Gold Awards (1997), *114*

Scott, Rory, 30

Settelen, Peter, 91, 99, 120

Shand Kydd, Peter (stepfather), 24, 40, 43, 80, 123

Shand Kydd, Frances (Lady Spencer: mother), 19, *19*, 21, 23, 24, *25*, 37, 38, 40, 43, 80, 87, 106, 123, *138*, 157

Silfield School, Gayton, 39–40

Simmons, Simone, 15, 17, 86, 92, 122

Skipwith, Michael, 103

Slater, Simon, 103

Sleep, Wayne, 83

Smith, Lady Abel, 30

Snowdon, Lord, *60*, *82*, 86

Soames, Catherine, *100*, 103

Soames, Nicholas, 84, 85, 103

Spencer, Charles, 9th Earl Spencer (brother), 11, *18*, 19, 20, *20*, 21, 23, 29, 38, 39, *39*, 40–1, *40–1*, 80, 129, *142–4*, *147*, 157

Spencer, Countess (grandmother), 120

Spencer, 7th Earl (grandfather), 120

Spencer family, 13, 19–24, *25*

Spencer, Frances, Countess *see* Shand Kydd

Spencer, Lady Jane *see* Fellowes

Spencer, John, 8th Earl (father), 8, 13, *19*, 21, 23, 26, 37, 43, *46*, 46–7, 122–3; death (1992), 37, 38, 73; divorce (1969), 13, 19

Spencer, John (brother), 23

Spencer, Raine, Countess (stepmother), *37*, 37–8, 39, 47, 131

Spencer, Lady Sarah, *see* McCorquodale

Spencer, Lady Victoria, 38

Spencer House, *117*

Stambolian, Christina, 110, *111*

Starzewski, Tomasz, 107, 115

Stevens, Muriel, 126

Swannell, John, 63–4, *148*

T

Tang, David, 103

Taylor, Iris, 129

Tchaikovsky, Peter, 15

Tetbury, near Highgrove, *33*

Thatcher, Margaret and Denis, 47

Thornton, Penny, 120

Thorpe Park, 68, 69

Toffolo, Joe and Oonagh, 125

U

United States, Diana in, *102*, *110*, 111, *112*, 126, 128

V

Van der Post, Sir Laurens, 14, 52, 75

Versace, Gianni, 107, *108*, *110*, 111, *114*, 115

Victoria, Queen, 47

Vogue, 106, 108, 113

W

Wakeley, Amanda, *115*

Wake-Walker, Elizabeth, 23

Waldner, Diane de (Mrs Hoare), 96

Wales, Royal visit to, 53, 55, *55*

Walker, Catherine, 107, *107*, *109*, 113, *114*, *115*

Wallace, Anna, 30

Ward-Jackson, Adrian, 66

West Heath School, Kent, 26

Westminster Abbey, 144; Diana's funeral in, 137, *138*, *144*, 157

Wetherby School, West London, 66

Whitaker, Alexandra, 30

Whitaker, Major Jeremy, 30

Whitaker, Philippa, 30

Whitelaw, Willie, 47

William, Prince, 8, *9*, 11, 15, *15*, *17*, 53, 55, *57*, 58, *60*–2, 63–4, 64–7, 66, 68, 70, *70–1*, 81–2, 85, 86, 87, 92, 95, 99, 131, *133*, 134, *137*, 138, 141, 142, *142–4*, 144, *148–9*, *149–50*, *151–2*, 153, *154–60*, 156–60; birth (1982), 15–16, *56*, 57–8, *59*, 60

Wimbledon, (1991), 67

Windsor, Duchess of, 134

Windsor, Edward, Duke of, 120, 134

Windsor, Combermere Barracks, 92; polo match (1992), *97*; Smith's Lawn, 16, *56*, 132

Windsor Castle, 13–14, 96, 158

Windsor Great Park, 16, *81*

Y

Yacoub, Sir Magdi, 97

Young England Kindergarten, Pimlico, 30, 40, 79

ACKNOWLEDGMENTS

While every effort has been made to trace copyright holders for photographs featured in this book, the publishers will be glad to make proper acknowledgment in future editions of this publication in the event that any regrettable omissions have occurred by the time of going to press.

Tim Graham: 12, 13, 14, 16, 31, 34, 44, 51, 55, 57, 61 (all), 62, 72, 89, 107 (left), 110, 111, 116 (top & bottom right), 126–7, 136, 149, 152, 154 (all except bottom right), 155 (all except second left, bottom), 158 (right), 163; Rex Features: 17, 28, 32, 48 (left), 50, 53, 54, 74, 76–77, 78, 90, 106, 116 (centre bottom), 117 (top left, centre top & centre bottom), 145 (right), 154 (bottom right), 155 (second left, bottom), 157, 159; Alpha: 6, 15, 20 (centre left), 33 (bottom), 80, 85, 108 (left), 113 (left), 116 (centre top), 117 (right), 124; Big Pictures: 56 (Ken Goff); 105, 114 (bottom right), 131, 132, 133; Camera Press: 42, 48–9, 59, 60, 148; All Action: 33 (top), 45, 70, 92 (left), 93 (bottom right), 116 (left); *Daily Mail*: 10 (bottom), 19, 20–1 (centre), 21 (bottom right), 22 (right), 25 (bottom right), 29, 40–41, 66, 75, 81 (bottom), 82, 84 (top), 87, 91, 96–7 (Mike Hollist), 107 (right), 109, 112 (right), 119, 123, 142–3, 144–5; Alan Davidson: 38; 'PA News': 8, 36, 39 (left), 115 (right), 118, 129, 138 (top), 138–9, 146, 147; Desmond O'Neil: 35; Lynn News: 20 (top left & bottom left); Richard Kay: 25 (bottom left); Photographers International: 9, 52; John Swannell: 64–65, back cover; Sygma: 7, 63, 71 (bottom), 102, 130, 150; Popperfoto: 47, 67; UK Press: 2, 69, 81 (top), 88, 94, 95, 98, 99, 100, 101, 108 (centre), 112 (left), 113 (centre), 114 (left & top right), 115 (left), 151, 153, 160, back cover; Lesley Donald: 71 (top); Nikos: 92–3, 117 (bottom left); Huw Evans: 93 (bottom left); New York Post: 93 (centre bottom); Nunn Syndication: 107 (centre), 113 (right); Popperfoto/ Reuters: 10 (top), 79, 115 (centre), 128, 137, 139 (top left & centre top); Patrick Demarchelier: cover, 104; *Daily Express*: 84 (bottom), 156; *Daily Mirror*: 43, 120; *News of the World*: 121; London Features International: 39 (right); Associated Press: 125; Eliot Press (Jason Fraser): 134–5; AFP: 140–1; NPA: 139 (top right); South West Pictures: 158 (left); Reginald Davis: 46.